NEW TRENDS IN MORAL THEOLOGY

NEW TRENDS IN MORAL THEOLOGY

A Survey of Fundamental Moral Themes

by

George M. Regan, C.M.

NEWMAN PRESS
New York / Paramus / Toronto

ACKNOWLEDGMENT

The quotations from Vatican Council II have been taken from *The Documents of Vatican II,* ed. Walter M. Abbott, S.J., The America Press, © 1966. Biblical quotations are from *The Jerusalem Bible,* Doubleday & Company, © 1966.

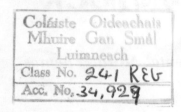
NIHIL OBSTAT:
John P. Whalen
Censor Librorum

IMPRIMATUR:
✠ Edwin B. Broderick, D.D.
Bishop of Albany

June 23, 1971

The Nihil Obstat and Imprimatur are official declarations that a book or pamphlet is free of doctrinal or moral error. No implication is contained therein that those who have granted the Nihil Obstat and Imprimatur agree with the contents, opinions or statements expressed.

Library of Congress
Catalog Card Number: 72-171102

Published by Newman Press
Editorial Office: 1865 Broadway, N.Y., N.Y. 10023
Business Office: 400 Sette Drive, Paramus, N.J. 07652

Printed and bound in the
United States of America

Contents

To
my mother and father,
sister and brother

Preface

Catholic moral theology has borne the brunt of considerable criticism in recent years. For a time, it seemed almost fashionable among theologians to decry the unrenewed and lamentable state of this theological enterprise. Complaints about the situation, however, outweighed positive contributions toward renewal. Biblical studies and dogmatic theology progressed, while moral theology stagnated.

Moral theologians have gradually responded to this challenge and emerging trends can now be discerned. Specialists recognize a need to reintegrate moral theology with God's Word in Sacred Scripture and with dogmatic theology, to replace its decidedly legalistic tone with the vitalizing force of Christian charity, to harmonize modern philosophical and theological trends with more traditional approaches, and to utilize better the insights of the behavioral sciences. General agreement exists that the academic isolation of moral theology must cease.

Confusion nevertheless exists in many quarters about the product of these new emphases, so unfamiliar to many clergy and laity alike. The difficulty is compounded in an era when the secular world has propounded a New Morality which espouses a freedom considered dangerous and alarming. The honest question of not a few asks whether Catholic moral theology has accepted this New Morality which verges on a new sexuality in the popular mind. Renewed moral theology, as a consequence, may yet gain more critics than the unrenewed version of a few years ago.

New Trends in Moral Theology will introduce the reader to some basic themes of Christian morality which enter into today's debates. Effort has been made to present a coherent point of view which may assist concerned Christians in sorting through the variety of opinions offered these days. I have attempted to synthesize and simplify the writings of many contemporary theologians found in technical journals and books in the hope of offering a balanced approach to a renewed moral theology and of stimulating the reader to delve into the literature himself. Students of theology in colleges, seminaries or training programs in religious education may find the work especially helpful. For this reason, references have been placed in the text itself and ample specialized bibliographies have been provided. A more profound view of each topic discussed can thus more readily be consulted.

1. The Nature of Moral Theology

Jesus challenges us by confronting us with divine revelation in his person and in his message. Faith in Jesus and the moral conversion to which that faith leads form an inseparable unity. The term "lived faith" aptly describes this reality, for it clearly states that God's self-gift precedes moral demands. (See J. Jeremias, *The Sermon on the Mount* [Philadelphia: Fortress, 1963] 34.)

This unity between religious doctrine and moral living establishes the radical possibility of a Christian moral theology. Christian living should follow from the manifestation reaching man through Jesus. Any attempt to interpret his preaching as a mere criticism of the civilization of his age, or as a humanistic program of social reform similar to those elaborated by ethicians, is wrong from the outset. A new and decisive divine revelation in the person of Jesus of Nazareth underlies his moral message. Conversion therefore implies more than a revision of one's moral behavior. Jesus announces the coming of the Kingdom in his person. God's self-communication demands a response. Man must open himself to a new message and prepare to relinquish his own way of thinking (Lk. 18:17; Mt. 19:15).

Jesus' moral preaching conserved many existing teachings of the Old Testament, and yet it was startlingly new. He did not elaborate a systematic development of moral duties, but his message is concrete and authoritative (Mt. 7:29; Mk. 1:22). His teaching often started from questions addressed to him by individuals, and his answers called for immediate life-decisions. "The people were so astonished that they started asking each other what it all meant. 'Here is a teaching that is new,' they said, 'and with authority behind it: he gives orders even to unclean spirits and they obey him" (Mk. 1:27).

3

Early Christianity reflected and built on this moral message of Jesus, adhering to its main lines and applying it to new problems as they arose. Christian reflection on and application of Jesus' teaching to daily living developed over the centuries into the theological discipline called "moral theology."

REFLECTION ON REVELATION

Moral theology studies in a scientific and organized fashion God's revelation of himself to man in Christ as an invitation which demands man's response by his free behavior. It emphasizes how men should behave and live. This study of the Christian way of life develops with special reliance on the teaching authority of Christ now exercised in the Church. (See E. McDonagh, "Moral Theology Renewed," *Irish Ecclesiastical Record* 104 [1965] 321-32.)

The proper context of moral theology embraces the salvation-redemption revealed in Christ and accepted by the Christian in faith. In a methodical and systematic fashion, it attempts to understand and apply this core content of revelation. It proposes Christian doctrine as truth to be lived and not only believed. St. Paul's words apply: "I want only the perfection that comes through faith in Christ, and is from God and based on faith. All I want is to know Christ and the power of his resurrection and to share his sufferings by reproducing the pattern of his death" (Phil. 3:9-10). Moral theology reflects primarily, therefore, on the revelation by which the triune God, in Christ and through his Church, manifests himself to us.

As a part of theology, moral theology studies primarily God, insofar as he invites man to share in his general plan for salvation in Christ. It studies also the free acts of man in his response to God's invitation. One can appreciate the broad context proper to moral theology, for it includes all human and created values and norms based on God's revelation and their consequences for Christlike living. Its ambit extends from revelation about man's destiny and personal dignity before God, to such specific applications as war, racial justice, abortion, lying, and divorce.

As a reflection in faith on God's Word, moral theology has as its ultimate principle faith, by which we accept the mystery of Christ our Savior. Reason serves in the explanation of this revelation grasped in faith. The moral teachings proposed in Sacred Scripture itself should occupy a central place in any presentation of Christian morality. The light of revelation should guide reason in searching out the practical and relevant consequences of God's Word for today's problems.

Moral theology should employ knowledge gained from human experience and from all branches of inquiry, especially psychology, medicine, sociology and philosophy. Neglect of empirical science leads to abstractionism and ivory-tower approaches to people's lives. For example, how can one evaluate the morality of the relatively new intrauterine devices (IUD's) for birth regulation without knowing how they function? Do they cause an abortion or do they hinder fertilization? Medical and biological science, not moral theology, provides the answers to these questions. The moralist evaluates the scientific facts in reaching his conclusion about the morality of such interventions. Even in treating these intricate questions, the Christian theologian ultimately reflects on the concrete implications of the salvation-redemption announced in Christ.

RELATION TO ETHICS AND
OTHER THEOLOGICAL DISCIPLINES

Ethics

Moral theology differs essentially in sources of knowledge, content, objectives and methodology from philosophical ethics. Catholic ethicians adhere to this distinction. Protestants often show the distinction by using the term "theological ethics" for what most Catholics term "moral theology." In an ethics course, one does not consider man's exalted destiny in Christ, Jesus' saving activity in his death, resurrection and ascension, nor God's graceful presence and assistance.

Philosophical ethics views man as he really exists, but only as known from man's personal and collective experiences accumulated through the centuries. These data of experience serve as the basis for the ethician's quest to discover man's destiny and the means which lie at his disposal. The entire dimension of God's Word spoken in Christ and in revelatory events remains outside its scope. Ethics cannot then embrace full reality and is basically imcomplete. (See R. McCormick, "Specificity of Christian Morality," *Theological Studies* 32 [1971] 71-78, for a discussion of different views on the possibly distinctive character of the Christian ethic.)

"Because there is in fact no such thing as a purely natural man, but only man in the concrete—the descendant of Adam, redeemed in Christ and called to a supernatural destiny—on theological grounds we must reject a purely immanent ethics of reason that would make itself absolute: it contradicts revelation" (F. Böckle, *Fundamental Concepts of Moral Theology* [Paramus, N.J.: Paulist Press, 1968] 4). Moral theology can, on the other hand, incorporate the insights of an ethics which treats man's moral project in the light of reason, while remaining open to faith. In manifesting himself in Christ, God does not contradict man's created endowment. A philosophical ethics which bases itself on man's moral ability founded in God's created gifts can contribute to moral theology many valid reflections which must then be integrated into a higher unity. Examples would be traditional and modern views of natural law, contemporary thought on contextualism, or the contemporary notion of responsibility. Theological writings on these areas often have their roots in philosophical ethics. (See G. Outka-P. Ramsey [ed.], *Norm and Context in Christian Ethics* [N.Y.: C. Scribner's, 1968]; A. Jonsen, *Responsibility in Modern Religious Ethics* [Washington, D.C.: Corpus, 1968].)

Dogmatic Theology

Dogmatic theology and moral theology constitute systematic theology, which reflects upon the totality of God's self-manifestation in Christ. These disciplines seek a deeper understanding of God's Word and are essentially one whole. Older theologians such as St. Thomas Aquinas in the *Summa Theologica* dealt with systematic theology as one science and made no distinction between dogmatic and moral theology. The two disciplines were later separated, especially after the Council of Trent (1545-1563). The study of the moral life was assigned to practical or moral theology and the remainder to speculative or dogmatic theology. This distinction was eventually crystallized to an excessive extent and modern complaints have stressed the deleterious effects. The mystery of Christ must penetrate moral theology and not be relegated to dogmatic theology.

For practical reasons, both disciplines continue to be taught separately, though the formerly sharp distinctions have lessened. The great increase in theological writings necessitates a procedure allowing specialization and ease of study. Today's teachers and students of moral theology must, however, remain aware of developments in dogmatic theology. Vatican II's *Pastoral Constitution on the Church in the Modern World* provides an outstanding example of the beneficial results of collaboration between moral and dogmatic theologians who addressed themselves to such broad problems as contemporary atheism, the theological meaning of human activity in this world, the dignity of the human person, and the significance of Christian marriage in Christ's saving mission. (See J. Fuchs, "Moral Theology and Dogmatic Theology," in *Human Values and Christian Morality* [Dublin: Gill and Macmillan, 1970], for a full treatment of this question.)

Ascetical Theology

Until rather recently, many theologians viewed moral theology as the science concerned with obligations, laws, sins and "ordinary" virtue. They relegated the study of "the higher stages of the spiritual life," the evangelical counsels and various mystical states to ascetical theology. Moral theology thus restricted itself mostly to the elaboration of universal moral principles and their application to particular cases. Ascetical theology treated the formation of conscience according to the personal and individual guidance of the Holy Spirit.

This conception of moral and ascetical theology resulted in a denigrated presentation of Christian moral ideals. Moral theology in this perspective must of necessity appear minimalistic, legalistic and obligationistic—in short, unevangelical. Protestant authors formerly criticized moral theology for this exact reason.

In recent times, many Catholics have joined in clamoring for reform in this area and many fine advances have occurred.

On the level of principle, any such separation between the obligatory and the ideal for Christian living must fail. If one conceives moral theology as a discipline which reflects on the implications of the call of man in Christ, one sees the narrow restrictiveness of considering it as the study of laws and sins alone. By omitting mention of the personal guidance of the Holy Spirit, one would eliminate a principal element of moral theology based on the New Testament.

For teaching purposes, a course in moral theology may only describe in a formal way the personal guidance of the Holy Spirit and leave to ascetical theology the study of the concrete ways of discerning the individual call of the Holy Spirit.

Canon Law

Moral theology embraces the total response of the Christian to God's invitation. Its content and interest therefore range far beyond the confines of Canon Law, which concerns Church laws made for the common good. If one were to rest content with explanations of the determinations of Canon Law concerning many moral questions, one might well present a minimalistic morality. The stress on the observance of Church law without a correlative exposition of the dynamism and the lofty ideals of New Testament morality may lead to a deplorable legalism, tending toward satisfaction with external conduct instead of internalized values. The Pharisees provide the classic type resulting from this thinking.

Moral theology should discuss some questions which have a close relationship with Canon Law, for example, the Christian attitude toward authority in the Church and toward ecclesiastical laws, and the correct way of approaching all human laws. It should avoid treating material on the specifics of Church laws (e.g., any commentary on canons in the Code of Canon Law).

SOURCES OF MORAL THEOLOGY

Sacred Scripture

W. Crotty, "Biblical Perspectives in Moral Theology," *Theological Studies* 26 (1965) 574-96.

R. Schnackenburg, *The Moral Teaching of the New Testament* (N.Y.: Herder & Herder, 1965).

J. Fuchs, "Moral Theology according to Vatican II," in *Human Values and Christian Morality* (Dublin: Gill and Macmillan, 1970) 25-37.

E. Hamel, "L'usage de l'Ecriture Sainte en théologie morale," *Gregorianum* 47 (1966) 53-85.

The *Dogmatic Constitution on Divine Revelation* states the following about the relationship between Sacred Scripture and theology: "Sacred theology rests on the written Word of God, together with sacred tradition, as its primary and perpetual foundation. By scrutinizing in the light of faith all truth stored up in the mystery of Christ, theology is most powerfully strengthened and constantly rejuvenated by that Word. For the Sacred Scriptures contain the Word of God and, since they are inspired, really are the Word of God; and so the study of the sacred page is, as it were, the soul of sacred theology" (n. 24).

The *Decree on Priestly Formation* makes the following explicit remarks about moral theology: "Special attention needs to be given to the development of moral theology. Its scientific exposition should be more thoroughly nourished by scriptural teaching. It should show the nobility of the Christian vocation of the faithful, and their obligation to bring forth fruit in charity for the life of the world" (n. 16).

Vatican II thus views Sacred Scripture as the *nourishment* of moral theology and as the *soul* of all sacred theology, terms which indicate how close the relationship should be. Sacred Scripture does not merely serve as just another argument or proof for some moral principles and particular norms. It should constitute the basic source giving moral theology its main orientation. In this way, moral theology retains contact with the mystery of Christ and God's revealed ways of dealing with men.

This starting point, orientation and perspective have obvious practical implications for moral theology today. For example, theologians who present the proper Christian attitude toward law cannot be content with Aristotle's notions or even those of contemporary philosophers of law. Using Sacred Scripture as a primary source, one must show how law relates to Jesus' preaching on the love of God and man, and to the theology of grace and justification. He will likewise find a great difference between Jesus' challenge in the Sermon on the Mount ("Be perfect as my heavenly Father is perfect") and non-Christian ethical doctrine on "the virtuous man." Moral theology has often labored under a confusion on such fundamental issues.

Biblical moral theology can greatly assist in the renewal of scientific moral theology. This theology proceeds beyond the faithful rendering and exegesis of texts to a comparison of various passages and themes. It aims at attaining a deeper sense of the meaning of Sacred Scripture. Biblical moral theology (e.g., Schnackenburg) does not, however, constitute the fullness of moral theology, for several reasons: first, theology must present not only the biblical data, but also a theological reflection on and elaboration of the revealed data; second, Sacred Scripture contains neither a theoretical system of Christian morality nor a synthesis of principles and values which apply to moral questions which arise in man's history; and third, not all elements in biblical moral theology have immediate importance in presenting the Christian moral message.

Certain errors must be avoided in the use of Scripture. Theologians may be tempted to consider the Bible as an arsenal in which they can search for the proof of a thesis they already hold. They may string together texts and gather scriptural citations which form a more or less disparate unity, without sufficiently sifting through historical and exegetical nuances. In effect, Scripture would be used to confirm an individual's personal reflections. Similar temptations may arise to give moral theology a scriptural flavor or to use Scripture only to edify.

The use of the Old Testament as a source for moral teaching is often most difficult and confusing. We sometimes lack criteria to distinguish between divinely revealed moral teaching and the opinions, customs and positive laws presented by the author. These particular views may not be the revelation itself that is offered for our belief. They serve in the transmission of God's message as the human vesture which allowed men of the Old Testament to communicate and to understand the divine Word. When doubt exists about the precise delineation between the substance and the vesture of Old Testament moral teaching, one does better to abstain from employing it in support of assertions. (For a positive statement of the valid content of Old Testament moral teaching, see W. Harrington, "The Law, the Prophets and the Gospel," in *Moral Theology Renewed*, ed, E. McDonagh [Dublin: Gill and Son, 1965] 31-54.)

The Teaching Authority of the Church

G. Baum, "The Magisterium in a Changing Church," *Concilium* 21 (1967), 67-83.
————, "Doctrinal Renewal," *Journal of Ecumenical Studies* 2 (1965) 365-81.
A. Dulles, "The Contemporary Magisterium," *Theology Digest* 17 (1969) 299-311.
D. Leigh, "The Church as a Moral Guide," *American Ecclesiastical Review* (1968) 385-98.
R. McCormick, "Morality and the Magisterium," *Theological Studies* 29 (1968) 707-18.
J. McKenzie, *Authority in the Church* (N.Y.: Sheed & Ward, 1966) 131-36.
K. Rahner, "Theology and the Magisterium after the Council," *Theology Digest* 16 (1968) 4-16.

The Church is a community of believers united by the Holy Spirit, who prolongs God's self-revelation in Christ through the work of men. Jesus himself is the Teacher in the Church. He teaches the Gospel which is not only a doctrine, but a way of life. Jesus carries on this teaching mission in the Church in many ways: in example and art, in the words of parents to their children, in sermons and catechesis, in conversation and discussions, in lectures and books, in pastoral letters and the declarations of popes and councils. The life-giving presence of the Holy Spirit guides and protects this total process in such a way that the Church as a whole cannot fail in her acceptance and proclamation of God's Word.

Among the various ways in which Jesus teaches, we may distinguish the continuous teaching office and the intermittent teaching office. By his continuous ministry of the Word, Jesus teaches in and through every baptized Christian. This takes place in conscientious action and witness, conversation and fraternal love in the daily lives of Christians. In a special way, he teaches in the celebration of God's Word in the liturgy. The ordained ministers of the Word promote and protect the prophetic mission of the Church, and all the faithful hear the power of God's Word. Related teaching, such as catechetics, which prepares for the liturgy, is also included in Jesus' continuous teaching. In a real sense, then, everyone in the Church bears a responsibility for the ongoing vitality of Jesus' continuing revelation in the Church.

This continuous ministry of the Word receives special help at times through statements to clarify points of Christian belief formulated by the whole college of bishops, with the pope as their head. These statements must always be viewed in the context of the entire Gospel, whose transmission has been given in a special way to the pope and to the bishops collectively. Vatican II summarizes this in the following way: "The task of authentically interpreting the Word of God, whether written or handed on, has been entrusted exclusively to the living teaching of the Church, whose authority is exercised in the name of Jesus Christ" (*Dogmatic Constitution on Divine Revelation,* n. 10). "Bishops are preachers of the faith who lead new disciples to Christ. They are authentic teachers, that is, teachers endowed with the authority of Christ, who preach to the people committed to them the faith they must believe and put into practice. By the light of the Holy Spirit, they make that faith clear" (*Dogmatic Constitution on the Church,* n. 25).

These authentic teachers in the name of Jesus are within the Church, not apart from and above the Church. They are not themselves the sources of truth for the Church, nor the inspirers of the whole activity of teaching. From their position within the

Church they should seek solutions to problems that trouble the faith of the Church, speaking out on issues that involve the response of the faithful to the Gospel. (See *Dogmatic Constitution on Divine Revelation,* n. 10.)

The Church at large has a correlative responsibility to attend to the voice of the hierarchy. Indeed, when the magisterium, speaking through the whole college of bishops or simply through the pope, gives definitive voice to the faith as received and professed by the Church, the response of the individual must be full assent, for here the magisterium is infallible.

Generally, the declarations of the papal or episcopal teaching office on moral matters are not infallible definitions of faith. Some human and Christian values are universally accepted as perennial, for example, the value of love and the worth of individual persons. But all values, even love, are realized in concrete choices and situations. These situations may change, and man's understanding of them may significantly develop and deepen. Appeal to traditional teaching on specific moral issues (e.g., the just war, various problems in medical interventions) is, therefore, not decisive unless it is clear that no such changes or developments have occurred.

What is the appropriate response of the believer to the contemporary non-infallible teaching office? At the least, it is a response of open, sympathetic and conscientious attention and consideration, with a presumption in favor of the proposed teaching. If the members of the Church are seeking the truth in faithful dependence on the Word of God, and are aware of Jesus' active teaching role in the Church guided by his Spirit, such an open and reflective response serves to purify the Church's faith and practical conduct in the faithful. This open response frequently leads to general acceptance, and this constitutes an important indication of the truth of a proposed teaching. For the Holy Spirit operates everywhere in the Church, leading believers to an understanding and acceptance of God's Word. (See the statement of the faculty of Alma College, California, "Conscience and the Magisterium," *America* [1968] 162-64.)

Moral theology must clearly remain in direct contact with the teaching office of the Church in order to know the Word which Jesus continues to teach. Problems such as the proper response to *Humanae Vitae* or to statements of particular bishops or episcopal conferences should not occasion a closed-mindedness to the authentic teaching office as such, a great risk today.

Revelation to All the Earth

A growing impatience has arisen because of a too facile recourse to the Gospel, the Sermon on the Mount, brotherly love, in short, a recourse to faith and the Scriptures for specific answers to secular problems. Some ask: "Of what use is the Gospel in resolving such complicated and worldly questions as the problems of war and peace, the race problem, and the population question?" A mood of secularism pervades many theological works as a consequence of such questions. Secularism and secularization refer to the process and task of estimating the true value of man and the world within the framework of faith. Many desire that the authentic autonomy of worldly values and man's reason within a Christian framework receive greater prominence in theological expositions. (See C. van Ouwerkerk, "Secularism and Christian Ethics," *Concilium* 25 [1967] 97-139; J. Fuchs, *Human Values and Christian Morality,* 112-47.)

God speaks to man not only in the Scriptures, the Church and the liturgy, but through his created works and through events. This natural revelation, as grasped by man's reason assisted by his faith, manifests many realities not mentioned in Scripture and other immediately theological sources. Earthly values have a continuing validity within the one totality of a living faith, for the "God of revelation" does not contradict the "God of creation." (See G. Moran, *Theology of Revelation* [N.Y.: Herder & Herder 1966] 162-78.) Indeed, one can agree with those contemporary authors who claim that the light of the Gospel helps us to discover the authentically human, but does not lead to something distinct from the material content of human morality discoverable by reason. Most moral teachings proposed in Catholic moral theology are not, in fact, drawn from purely Christian sources, but rather stem from rational reflection on the way of living and behavior that corresponds best to the human person in his concrete manhood.

The Teaching of the Fathers and Theologians

The Church has always esteemed greatly the early writers called the Fathers. Vatican II speaks in this vein: "The words of the holy Fathers witness to the living presence of this tradition, whose wealth is poured into the practice and life of the believing and praying Church" (*Dogmatic Constitution on Divine Revelation,* n. 8). The value of the Fathers' writings is one of witness to the authentic belief of the Church as a whole. The unanimous teachings of theologians likewise merit respect as valuable sources of authentic Christian witness to Christian belief, when proposed uninterruptedly in full acceptance by the Christian community. (For a recent treatment of this complex question, see R. McCormick, "The Teaching Role of the Magisterium and of Theologians," CTSA *Proceedings* 24 [1969] 239-54.)

A word of caution might be added about the use of the writings of the Fathers and theologians. The history of moral theology shows that opinions once espoused by writers over several centuries were obviously incorrect. Theological opinions concerning the licit use of torture to exact confessions for crimes or concerning the justice of slavery may serve as examples of outstanding errors. Great difficulty therefore exists in citing some teachings proposed by the Fathers and theologians.

2. Historical Survey of Moral Theology

All theology is rooted in history, for it represents the community's reflection on God's self-gift in Christ. The history of moral theology has not been one of unstemmed progress in penetrating the implications of this central mystery. It underwent extended periods of decadence and erroneous teachings, some of which severely distorted the Christian message. An overall look at the historical background of present-day moral theology may prove worthwhile in assessing the task of contemporary Christians who strive to make relevant the teaching of Jesus.

R. Dailey, "New Approaches to Moral Theology," in *Current Trends in Theology,* ed. D. Wolf-J. Schall (Garden City: Image Books, 1966) 162-89.

J. Ford-F. Kelly, *Contemporary Moral Theology,* Vol. I (Paramus, N.J.: Newman, 1958) chap. 5-6.

B. Häring, *The Law of Christ,* Vol. I (Paramus, N.J.: Newman, 1961) 3-33.

THE MORAL TEACHING OF THE NEW TESTAMENT

J. Blank, "Does the New Testament Provide Principles for Modern Moral Theology? *Concilium* 25 (1967) 9-22.

C. H. Dodd, *Gospel and Law* (N.Y.: Columbia University Press, 1951).

J. Jeremias, *The Sermon on the Mount* (Philadelphia: Fortress Press, 1963).

T. W. Manson, *Ethics and the Gospel* (London: SCM Press, 1960).

17

R. Schnackenburg, *Christian Existence in the New Testament*, 2 vols. (Notre Dame Univ., 1968, 1969.)
————, *The Moral Teaching of the New Testament* (N.Y.: Herder & Herder, 1965).
C. Spicq, *Théologie morale du Nouveau Testament* (Paris: Gabalda, 1965).

The moral teaching of the New Testament is embedded in a context which consists of a report of historical facts and an explanation of their religious significance, and this fact gives to Christian morality a peculiar character (cf. Dodd, 8). This religious and historical context has prime importance for understanding New Testament ethics. In the earliest period of Christianity, preachers of the new religion worked out two distinctive forms of preaching, namely, proclamation (kerygma) and teaching (didache).

Proclamation concerned the message about the crucified and risen Lord and his return. In these events, God himself has acted decisively to inaugurate his kingdom on earth. "The time has come . . . and the kingdom of God is close at hand. Repent, and believe the Good News" (Mk. 1:15). The kerygma is thus the proclamation of Christ, the message that he has redeemed us and is our peace. "The oldest statement of the kerygma is to be found in 1 Cor. 15:3-5: Jesus died for our sins in accordance with the Scriptures and was buried. God raised him on the third day in accordance with the Scriptures, and he appeared to Cephas, then to the twelve" (Jeremias, 19-20).

In contrast to the proclamation, the teaching includes instructions for the Christian conduct of life. These instructions constantly repeated the proclamation and added teaching on morals, the sacraments, man's destiny (Heb. 6:2), and scriptural texts and information about the life of Jesus. "Based on the claim that God himself has personally intervened in the history of mankind to inaugurate his Kingdom on earth, this instruction urged those who had accepted the Christian proclamation to embark on a new way of life in which, through God's mercy, they would be relieved of their past sins and failings, and could enjoy a new relationship with God in Christ Jesus, dead and risen from the dead" (F. X. Murphy, *Moral Teaching in the Primitive Church*

[Paramus, N.J.: Paulist Press, 1968] 7). Examples of didache are found in Matt. 6:5-15 and Luke 11:1-13, which contain two instructions on prayer. "The Sermon on the Mount as a whole is, together with the Epistle of James, the classical example of an early Christian didache" (Jeremias, 22).

The authors of the New Testament faced an historical situation which greatly influenced the content and purpose of these writings. While Jesus pursued his ministry in person, he often reproached his hearers because they had the wrong attitude toward God and to their fellow men, and he tried to bring them to a different attitude. That situation had passed and Jesus had suffered, died and risen. The Christian community recalled his sayings and doings and found ways of applying what had been said to Jesus' listeners, for example, the scribes and Pharisees, to their own case (Manson, 101). Jesus' attitudes and practical ways of acting formed as important a part of this Christian heritage as did his words.

In the Gospels particularly, we are witnesses of a process by which the day-to-day answers of Jesus, his ways of dealing with the particular concrete situations that arose during his ministry, are turned into the moral insights of the Church. This process appears most clearly in the parables, which originally had their own actual situations in the life of Jesus. Each was once uttered by Jesus on a day, in a set of circumstances and to a definite group of people. By the time they were included in the Gospel, many were invested with a new situation in the life of the early Church and adapted to the theological purpose of the evangelist. The early Christians did not, then, simply invent their moral doctrines. They drew from the mass of Jesus' sayings what they considered relevant for the teaching of the faithful, that is, for forming the didache. Besides this heritage, they gathered further insights not directly transmitted in the preserved sayings of Jesus and each evangelist used all this material to highlight his particular perspective of the Gospel. (See C. H. Dodd, *The Parables of the Kingdom,* chap. 4; J. Jeremias, *The Parables of Jesus,* 20-38.)

This teaching in the Gospels centers on the sovereign majesty of God breaking into human affairs in the person of Jesus. In his Son, the Father accepts the world and reconciles estranged man to himself. Jesus came as the culmination of God's promises spoken throughout his dealings with his chosen people. In Jesus, by him, and with him we become sons of God, and return as sons to the Father from whom our sins have alienated us. The call to conversion and salvation centers in Jesus, who manifests the love of the Father. The didache based on this Gospel message depicts Jesus as proposing a new law to his disciples. Though he restates and refines the Ten Commandments revealed through Moses, he goes further: "Be perfect as your heavenly Father is perfect" (Matt. 5:48). "I give you a new commandment: love one another; just as I have loved you, you also must love one another. By this love you have for one another, everyone will know that you are my disciples" (John 13:34-35). New Testament morality is not codified into an elaborate system, but rather states general outlines and fundamental attitudes for practical living, all animated by love. Jesus speaks of life in him, following in his footsteps as disciples, loving service of one another, humility, and positive love of one's enemies. The eight Beatitudes of the Sermon on the Mount epitomize Jesus' message (Matt. 5:3-11). The moral life of Christians should, therefore, escape emphasis on law. It basically consists in a morality of love, a personal, loving response to God's self-gift in Jesus. This divine call requires a wholehearted yes. A Christian who fully answers God will focus on the person of Jesus, "the way, the truth and the life" (John 14:6). "The proclamation of the eschatological event calls for repentance; the act of God in the Gospel constitutes an appeal to man for a better life: the gift and the demand are inseparable" (W. Davies, *The Sermon on the Mount* [Cambridge, 1966] 137).

The Christian lives immersed in history and events. Many concrete moral problems arose in the early Church which clamored for authoritative solutions by Jesus' disciples. Not satisfied with sheer pragmatism as a pertinent solution, these early leaders based their teaching on moral insights based consistently on Jesus' teaching and deeds. The moral preaching contained in sermons and the letters of the apostles re-echoes the Gospel message. The basis for this preaching remains the same as found in the Gospels: the love of the Father for all men; the mystery of the Incarnate Word; the role of the Holy Spirit, sent by Jesus; and the gift of grace, whereby we become other Christs and with him return to the Father. Repentance and conversion follow from these realities. This appears clearly in St. Peter's speech in Acts 2:14-42, a description of the coming of the gift of the Holy Spirit to the new community on Pentecost. The question of salvation has become urgent in Jesus, whom God has raised from the dead to his right hand. Having received the promise of the Spirit from the Father, he has poured out what Peter's listeners see and hear. Peter bases his practical application on this entire event: "You must repent . . . and every one of you must be baptized in the name of Jesus Christ for the forgiveness of your sins, and you will receive the gift of the Holy Spirit. . . . Save yourselves from this perverse generation" (Acts 2:38, 40).

St. Paul repeatedly views the specific marks of a life regulated entirely according to the Gospel as living in union with Christ and in fraternal charity. The Christian must respond in love to the love with which God and Christ first loved us (cf. Eph. 5:2). In his mind, all activity should be seen as a building up of a new temple of God in each Christian, a new creation, and a new perfection of the image of God existing in each man. Joined to Christ as a new people of God, each Christian has the duty to live according to the pattern of Christ. "Be what you already are" summarizes Paul's basic moral principle. For this reason, he rebukes the early Christian communities for their failures in morality and lists principal sins in his so-called catalogues of vices. (See C. Spicq, *The Trinity and Our Moral Life According to St. Paul* [Paramus, N.J.: Newman, 1963].)

These reflections of St. Paul and the early Christian community constitute the real beginnings of moral theology. Though unsystematic, they fulfill an essential aspect of moral theology, for they attempt to understand and apply Christian belief to practical living.

THE PRIMITIVE CHURCH

F. X. Murphy, *Moral Teaching in the Primitive Church* (Paramus, N.J.: Paulist Press, 1968).

————, "The Background to a History of Patristic Moral
Thought," in *Studia Moralia,* Vol. I (Rome: Ancora, 1962)
49-85.

Toward the end of the first century, the early Church initiated
more intense reflection on the moral message of Jesus. The primary concern was to ensure faithful adherence to the primitive
Christian heritage. One finds a relatively simple moral catechesis
which arranged in summary and sketchy form the moral instructions found in the Old and New Testaments or in the sayings of
Jesus handed down in oral tradition. The moral duty of the Christian, briefly stated, is to believe in Christ and to follow him without reserve. "What is characteristic of the primitive Christian
communities, of course, is the insistence on Christ's charity—his
'compassion for the multitudes.' This was translated into loving
one's neighbor as one's self in Christ, and was noticed by their
pagan and Jewish contemporaries: 'See how these Christians love
one another'" (Murphy, 114). The early writings also show the
initial phases of the basic outlines later adapted in moral theology: the teaching on virtue as the way of salvation in Christ,
and sin as the rejection of God's invitation in Christ.

Contemporary problems arose through the extension of Christianity into the surrounding Roman world, and by the growth and
development of the Church herself. Elements of the Stoic, Pla-
tonic and eclectic philosophies served as a focal point for the
application of Christian moral principles. Individuals took up the
major issues of the time, which usually dealt with worship to
pagan idols, martyrdom, or obedience to Church authority. They
addressed themselves to the proper Christian attitude toward the
theater, fashions, military service in the pagan army, cooperation
with the pagan State, and many other topics. "The Fathers did
have opinions on poverty, war, sex, divorce, slavery, virginity,
and scandal, but they would hardly have considered treating
them at length in separate analyses. These abstractions could only
be considered in the concrete situation in which the individual
Christian found himself" (Murphy, 1).

Whatever the topic, the Fathers ordinarily based their insights
and solutions on its relation to the following of Christ. Their

answers are not characterized by an escape or evasion of the difficulty through flight from the world itself, but by the more profound escape from the evils of the world by not being of the world, though remaining in the world.

LATER PATRISTIC TIMES:
THIRD TO SIXTH CENTURIES

The Fathers of this period treated quite profound questions, such as the relationship existing between the Christian law and pagan philosophy, and the supernatural character of Christian revelation and moral striving. St. Clement of Alexandria (died c. 216) made the first thorough effort to construct a truly systematic moral theology. He wrote extensively about free will, virtue, and vice, and presented Christ as the center and the ideal of authentic Christian life.

St. Augustine (354-431) may well be the greatest moral theologian of all time, even though he never composed a systematic work covering the whole of morality. His individual writings concentrate on specific questions, for example, marriage, virginity, widowhood, continence, lying, patience, and the theological virtues. His work as a whole merits recognition, moreover, for precisely those doctrinal problems are placed in the foreground which are basic to moral theology: grace and freedom, faith and good works, faith and love, original sin and restoration in grace, the natural law, and loving union with God in eternal happiness as the end-purpose of Christian morality. Though holding fast to certain basic values which he had absorbed from the teachings of Plotinus and Plato and from the ethics of the Stoics, Augustine succeeded for the most part in purifying this pagan thought by centering his moral theology in faith and love inspired by divine grace. Christian moral perfection resides in charity, which accomplishes the Law and sums up every virtue in itself. His teachings on all these areas have had a profound impact upon the whole history of Christian moral theology. Recent attacks made on the saint for his pessimism in sexual morality should not obscure his profound and original contributions to understanding the implications of Jesus' moral teaching. (See J. Noonan, *Contraception: A History of Its Treatment by the Catholic Theologians and Canonists* [Cambridge: Harvard University, 1965] Chapter IV.)

The Early Middle Ages:
Seventh to Twelfth Centuries

The period from 600 to 1200 was generally unproductive in original contributions to moral theology, mirroring in this way the general tenor of the age. Emphasis was laid upon the practical points made in the writings and the sermons of the Fathers, and on the decrees of popes, bishops, and councils issued to maintain the Christian moral ideal in the face of the moral excesses of the times.

The only original and creative sources during this period were the penitential books (*libri poenitentiales*). These handy compilations and summaries of moral doctrine had a singular significance for the later development of moral theology. They were composed to aid confessors, who were often insufficiently trained in theology, in determining the gravity of sins and in indicating appropriate sacramental penances to be imposed on various classes of penitents. Since nothing was left to the discretion of the individual priest-confessors, specific mortal sins receive minute attention. One penitential book actually listed twenty varieties of murder, assigning a proportionate penance for each. These catalogues of sins and penances assumed a primary practical importance for spiritual guidance, because expositions of a positively oriented moral theology were wanting. Largely mechanical in nature, they placed an excessive stress on sin and satisfaction for sin, disregarding the Christian ideal and many fundamental moral principles. They are the first example of an unfortunate tendency throughout the later history of moral theology, namely, the categorizing or codifying of morality by stressing abstract cases and sins, without due attention to their basis in moral principle.

The twelfth century introduced the era of the canonists. The rediscovery of Roman Law lent great importance to legal perspectives and Canon Law built on this foundation and also used conciliar and Patristic texts. The canonists discussed moral problems in their works, but within a juridical framework. They concentrated on the general principles of law, contracts, justice, sin, and the contractual nature of marriage. Instead of viewing Christian morality as essentially an ethic of love as proposed by Jesus and the early Church, the canonists taught a morality of law. One searches in vain for stress on God's loving invitation to man, who is called to respond in love through Christ. Religion and morality are, on the contrary, seen as a rather impersonal adherence to a moral code imposed from without. Duty and obligation attain primary importance at the expense of loving response in union with and imitation of Christ.

Moral theology has still not shaken off the influences of the canonists which began during this era. Textbooks on Catholic moral theology, articles, instruction, and preaching from our pulpits still echo the excessive stress on duty and obligation first voiced to an extreme in this decadent period. Though theology stood at the threshold of a golden age at the close of the twelfth century, a clearly defined moral theology remained wanting. Some great theologians instead reserved to theology only the study of God and the divine mysteries of our salvation-redemption, leaving to philosophy the study of practical morality, which was worked out with a strong accent on law. This defect first occurred in the twelfth century as a general failing and still exists today in some Catholic circles. Only within the past several decades can one detect serious and efficacious efforts to overcome this pernicious tendency which reduces Christian moral existence to the purely rational and philosophical level.

THE HIGH MIDDLE AGES: THIRTEENTH CENTURY

The Scholastics constructed lengthy syntheses of the doctrine about the faith called "Summas." Many authors, such as St. Albert the Great (1193-1280) and St. Bonaventure (1221-1274), devoted themselves almost exclusively to treating the great mysteries of our faith in a rather speculative manner, studying moral aspects only in connection with the doctrine on the creation, the fall of man, the incarnation, and the sacraments. While these treatises often provided valuable theological reflection, they failed to develop the relevancy of the Christian mysteries for concrete, daily moral life.

St. Thomas Aquinas (died 1274) provided notable beginnings for a science of moral theology explained within the context of the entire doctrine of faith. In his masterful synthesis, faith seeks understanding in the fullest sense. God as Creator and Christ as our Savior and Master form the foundation for the presentation of ideal Christ-like living. He places great emphasis on the role of natural reason as enlightened by grace in the discernment of criteria for moral activity. The teaching of Genesis about the natural image of God in man explains Thomas' stress on the continuing value of natural law and natural reason in the Christian economy of salvation. Though incorporating much Aristotelian terminology and methodology into his works, Thomas relied principally upon Sacred Scripture and traditional theology.

Thomas begins his treatment of moral questions only after explaining questions concerning God's existence, nature, and creative activity. Christian moral living is then considered as man's motion to God, his final goal in life, by means of free acts. Christ as man assists us in this ascent to God. Following his example and sustained by his gifts of grace won through his incarnation and redemptive activity, we are reborn, repaired, and made to grow. Christ's sacramental actions performed within the body of his elect, which is the Church, contribute vital sustenance for our moral life. Thomas' stress on the ecclesial nature of Christian activity thus safeguards his teaching from a harmful individualism. Our resurrection from the dead joins us finally to Christ and culminates our total journey to God.

The Thomistic exposition differs essentially from that of Aristotle in that man's self-perfection through his own powers no longer constitutes the core content and aim of moral striving. Love, openness to God, and response to grace and to the Word and example of Christ become the proper path for the Christian to travel. In this way, Thomas proposes Christian moral doctrine as a teaching centering upon God, who personally loves and cares for man, rather than as a teaching centering upon man and his attainment of personal happiness.

NOMINALISM: FOURTEENTH AND FIFTEENTH CENTURIES

The positive advances effected in the works of the great Scholastic theologians were almost eliminated in the succeeding two centuries, which were dominated by the metaphysics of William of Ockham (died 1359). The fundamental emphasis of his Nominalism fastened on the unique and exclusive value of the singular, the concrete, and the individual, which alone really exists. The basic orientation of Nominalism concentrated on the individual man and his individual acts, fostering thereby a moral system of individualism. In this view, only the single act merits consideration, since everything permanent, constant, or universal in scope is denied. Nominalism viewed morality as a succession of decisive acts. Interest was consequently focused unduly on the consideration of each particular decision with its unique meaning and precise circumstances, without due regard for the totality of moral endeavor. As a result, Nominalism paved the way for later developments of excessive "casuistry," that is, a study of various case-types of moral acts which occur with some frequency.

Besides this stress on individualism, Nominalism was decidedly voluntaristic in principle, granting to man's will an absolute power of self-determination, even independent of seemingly reasonable motivation. In the moral order, the "good" is whatever God freely and even arbitrarily desires to be good, and "law" is whatever God enjoins under obligation. God could even allow acts of outright blasphemy and consider them good. This stress on God's arbitrary thinking survived the demise of Nominalism and prevails, after a certain fashion, until the present day. As a further consequence, moral theology expressed less interest in positive Christian virtue than in law and the Commandments. The presentation of moral doctrine became a listing of "do's and don'ts" and correct moral endeavor took on the character of an impersonal carrying out of duties and obligations imposed by God.

The Protestant Reformers of the sixteenth century inherited much of their positive hatred for law from this harmful teaching of Ockham and Nominalism in general. One may even trace back to this same source the difficulties of modern Protestant theologians, who continue to see an opposition between Law and Gospel. When coupled with the continuing influence of Canon Law on moral theology, Nominalism lies at the root of much legalism and obligationism in Catholic moral theology. The general impact of Nominalism on the sound development of theology and on practical Christian living proved disastrous. On the positive side, Nominalism contributed to the knowledge of the individual moral act in its subjective and specifying aspects. The immense mass of data and observations on these questions furnished by the Nominalistic moralists of this period can be properly expurgated and incorporated with profit into the context of a more solid moral system, based on true Christian principles.

MORAL THEOLOGY A DISTINCT SCIENCE: SIXTEENTH CENTURY

This period witnessed a revival of St. Thomas' doctrine and the birth of moral theology as a distinct theological discipline divorced from dogmatic theology. The Thomistic revival contributed immeasurably to a well-organized and comprehensive treatment of moral problems on the speculative and practical levels. The best representatives of this renaissance embodied within a framework of Thomas' moral teaching the positive fruits of Nominalism, and made important advances in the study of justice and of the mutual rights of nations.

On the other hand, the separation of morals and dogma as distinct sciences worked havoc in the succeeding centuries. The traditional synthesis was now displaced almost entirely by a penchant for the practical and concrete, which made of moral theology an autonomous science with an exclusively practical orientation. Authors strove not so much to teach a positive moral science as to form correctly the consciences of the Christian faithful and to teach confessors the doctrinal principles underlying the correct solution of cases.

The practical problem to be solved is expressed in the question: Has this penitent sinned? Yes or no? In this presentation of morality, the primacy of honor was accorded to conscience, Law, sin, the Commandments of God and of the Church, the duties of particular states of life, and canonical penalties. The incorporation of much canonical legislation into the moral theology treatises, especially those on marriage and penance, became the standard practice. Empirical and self-contained, these works, called *Institutiones morales,* presupposed prior or complementary study of philosophy, dogmatic theology, spiritual theology, and speculative moral theology. Since they generally succeeded in supplying sound principles for casuistry, they enjoyed a great success.

PROBABILISM AND ST. ALPHONSUS:
SEVENTEENTH AND EIGHTEENTH CENTURIES

Divorced from dogmatic theology, moral theology pursued its own course of development and focused attention on the treatise concerning the judgment of conscience. Fervid controversies arose which principally concerned the problem of probabilism. (See R. Dailey, 175-77.)

The central difficulty can be summarized as follows: In a concrete decision to perform a moral act, a doubt frequently occurs whether to follow the law or to follow freedom. When a law clearly binds, a person must obey the law if he wishes to serve God. When no law exists, a person may act as he wishes without any offense to God. But what ought he do when uncertainty exists concerning the law? Is he bound to obey a doubtfully existing law? Is he bound to obey a law, if he doubts its valid application to the case at hand? Or rather, is he free to follow his own inclination with the practical certitude that he acts morally? In some way, the authors were concerned solely with an immediately practical question demanding an answer: sin or no sin? In this context, many doubts about the correct solution inevitably occurred. These controversies led to the formation of the various moral systems for forming a correct conscience through reflex moral principles.

This obsessive concern with moral certainty initiated a long period of decadence for moral theology. There eventually set in a rather basic sterility of the entire moral theological endeavor and a general disregard of the unique character of Christian morality. Harmful casuistry prevailed, which reduced morality to a carefully constructed system of foreordained conclusions based on universally valid, abstract principles. During the succeeding years, the history of moral theology might be characterized as the history of the moral system called "probabilism." Such limited horizons soon left moral theology as a devitalized and insipid discipline of the obligatory and the minimal. A certain trend toward laxism followed as a natural consequence.

During this extended period of decadence, the outstanding figure was St. Alphonsus Liguori. The saint compiled his moral treatise for the benefit of the Redemptorist seminarians, who as priests and missionaries were destined to direct Christian consciences. He sought to find a middle way between the rigorist and laxist tendencies of his own day. To achieve this goal, he carefully weighed and evaluated the opinions of all the leading moral authors on their own intrinsic merits, and then expressed his own opinion. In successfully accomplishing this purpose, Alphonsus saved the Church from the extremes of rigorism and laxism, and he earned the title "Patron of Confessors." It must, nevertheless, be conceded that the Alphonsian moral teaching remains in the mainstream of the moral theology prevalent since the end of the sixteenth century, partaking of its vigor and also of its weakness. (See B. Häring, "Is the Moral Theology of St. Alphonsus Relevant?" in *This Time of Salvation* [N.Y.: Herder & Herder, 1966] 53-72.)

MODERN TIMES: NINETEENTH AND TWENTIETH CENTURIES

In reaction to the rationalism of the enlightenment (*Aufklärung*), Johann Michael Sailer (1751-1832) and Johann Baptist von Hirscher (1788-1865) attempted a renewal and reformulation of a truly Christian moral theology, stripped of its juridicism and reintegrated into dogmatic theology. Sailer's principal work, *Manual of Christian Morality* (1818), cultivated the perfect ideal of the Christian way, which consists in continuous conversion and growth. In 1834, von Hirscher published his *Christian Moral Teaching as Realization of the Kingdom of God.* As the title indicates, this work purported to base morality on the theme of the Kingdom of God as presented in Sacred Scripture. Some have, therefore, labeled von Hirscher as the precursor of the return to the Bible in moral theology. However, von Hirscher's use of Scripture is more romantic than biblical, in accordance with the exegetical tendency of his age. His lack of familiarity with the Scholastics' moral theology and his opposition to the neo-Scholastic method also mar his work. (See E. Hamel, "L'usage de l'Ecriture Sainte en théologie morale," *Gregorianum* 47 [1966] 162-63.)

As the bitterness of the probabilist controversies gradually subsided, moral authors gravitated toward one or another of the principal moderate moral systems, probabilism, probabiliorism, and equi-probabilism. The manuals of moral theology used in seminaries until recently were composed toward the end of the last century and in the early part of the present century. The constant appearance of new editions of these works has partially fulfilled their chief purpose: to prepare seminarians for the pastoral charge of administering the sacrament of penance. Since these manuals treat mostly practical moral problems, in line with their purpose of preparing confessors, they generally attempt a reaffirmation and deepening of the moral principles of St. Alphonsus. At the same time, they manage to incorporate some speculative elements drawn from the Thomistic renaissance of the late nineteenth century.

The case for a needed renewal of moral theology is sometimes presented in a completely negative fashion, which consists in a direct criticism of the manuals. Only their more obvious and indisputable defects are listed in a damaging way without sufficient understanding of the historical purpose, development, and intrinsic merits of these works. Since most college textbooks of moral theology are patterned according to these manuals, criticisms of them imply criticisms of the college textbooks. One should consider both the positive and negative aspects of the manuals in order to understand the twentieth-century attempts at remedying the situation.

The positive aspects of the manuals have been well summarized as follows: "These manuals have great value. Although the matter which they present is awesome, it is logically ordered, clearly presented, and easily mastered. Basic in their structure are solid principles that provide a consistent and safe casuistry. In these manuals one finds the clear distinction between serious moral duties which cannot be ignored or violated and works of higher perfection to which man is called and invited by grace but not held to perform by strict obligation. Contained in the multiphasic exposition of duties are most of the moral, liturgical, rubrical, canonical, and pastoral precepts and problems which a priest is likely to meet in the pastoral and confessional ministry. Periodicals supplement every part of the manuals by presenting special writings on problems arising in psychology, medicine, law, business, marriage, education, politics, social order, and a host of other phases of human life. The manuals make these writings intelligible and usable, within the structure of moral theology. As it is taught today, moral theology leaves to ascetical and mystical theology, the literature of which is quantitatively enormous and qualitatively very good, the more detailed guidance of souls in the more perfect life. Moral theology is entirely consistent with the dogmatic theology which the seminarian studies during the four-year course of theology. Thanks to these manuals the priest upon leaving the seminary is able to enter without great difficulty upon his duties and to carry them out with a relatively high degree of effectiveness. Furthermore, he is open to whatever growth in pastoral perfection his experience might lead him" (R. Dailey, 179-80).

A general feeling of uneasiness about the decadent state of moral theology has crept into the writings of Catholic theologians, especially following World War II. In the United States, this reaction occurred with some strength in the mid-1950's and has continued until the present day. The strictures of contemporary critics should not be construed as mere murmurings of malcontents. They sincerely ponder the fact that "moralist" has sometimes connoted the censurious critic who spoils the fun by splitting hairs. They are repelled at the realization that the same term has connoted: "Consult so and so: he will get you out of anything if anyone can!" Whether the Catholic moralist be typified as a moral rigorist or as one tinged with moral laxity, the frequency of such caricatures indicates underlying dissatisfaction with the moral theology of past days. (See J. Ford-G. Kelly, *Contemporary Moral Theology*, Vol. I, 42-59, for a good description of the state of things in 1958.)

In recent years, these negative remarks have lost much of their validity, for a true renewal of moral theology has definitely begun. The critical opinions, moreover, often overlap and verge at times on being contradictory. Awareness of past deficiencies which have merited justifiable criticism should, however, aid students of Christian ethics in avoiding similar mistakes in future days.

These various criticisms may be conveniently grouped under two general headings: first, moral theology has become preponderantly a system of philosophical ethics and is not sufficiently in contact with the central mysteries of Christian belief; second, a classical world-view pervades Catholic moral theology, whereas contemporary man has adopted a more historically conscious and evolving world-view.

The first general criticism rightly implies that moral theology became effectively separated from basic points of God's revealed Word which were relegated to dogmatic theology. The central role of Christ in salvation and the sanctifying mission of the Holy Spirit failed to receive sufficient stress. The sacramental basis of Christian life, stemming from incorporation into Christ and the Church in baptismal consecration, did not serve as a starting principle. The scriptural sources of life in Christ were often cited only as supporting arguments for conclusions reached by reason.

Divorced from its vital Christian sources, moral theology pursued its own course and emerged in an unhealthy state. It became directed more to casuistry and inevitably seemed to endorse a certain minimalism. Excessive stress on sin, on the distinction between mortal and venial sin, and on the difference between precepts and counsels gave a negative tone to moral theology. Positive values tended to recede to the background and "thou shalt not" became prominent. Living within the confines of the law, whether natural law or human law, especially Canon Law, replaced the open-ended morality of love preached by Jesus. One would hardly offer a traditional seminary manual or many college textbooks on moral theology to interested Christians searching for the practical implications of the evangelical ideals. (See R. Dailey, 180-82.)

A second main criticism contends that the classicist world-view embodied in traditional moral theology has been replaced by a more historically conscious world-view. The classicist world-view emphasizes the static, the unchangeable, the eternal, and speaks in terms of substances and essences. Essences remain unchangeable and undergo only accidental modifications in the course of time. Its theological methodology is abstract, a priori and deductive, for it strives to gain insight into the abstract and universal essence and prescinds from accidental circumstances. This methodology underlies the familiar approach whereby the first principles of morality are first established and other universal norms of conduct are deduced from these. Since this classicist methodology has permeated moral theology, one naturally discovers in this discipline a stress on objective and unchanging standards. It would sometimes seem that moral theologians could answer any query by fitting it into pre-determined and neat categories. This tendency reduces the dynamic and inspirational message announced by Jesus to an abstract, static and torpid condition. The progressive and developing character of religious insight does not appear.

Traditional moral theology based on this classicist world-view proves greatly irrelevant for many contemporaries schooled in a more historical world-view. For them, the world appears as constantly evolving; progress, development and growth mark the world and man. Movement and a stress on subjectivity characterize this approach. Its theological methodology tends to be concrete, a posteriori and inductive. The concrete, particular and individual thing and person allow us to meet reality. Abstraction, unchangeableness and certitude cede to concreteness, change and tentativeness. Since accidental circumstances receive more prominence, the historical world-view remains more open to the data of the empirical sciences, notably psychology, sociology, and anthropology. (See R. Springer, "Conscience, Behavioral Science and Absolutes," in *Absolutes in Moral Theology?*, ed. C. Curran [Washington: Corpus, 1968] 19-56.)

In light of this clash between such diverse world-views, one may appreciate why many contemporaries claim that moral theology fails to answer their needs. Its basic world-view, content and language seem repellent. (See C. Curran, "Absolute Norms and Medical Ethics," in *Absolutes in Moral Theology?*, 125-45, for a fuller treatment of this changed world-view; also, I. Lobo, "Toward a Morality Based on the Meaning of History: The Condition and Renewal of Moral Theology," *Concilium* 25 [1967] 23-45.) Moral theologians have welcomed many of these criticisms, and have taken many steps to correct the deficiencies found in their branch of theology. This positive renewal of moral theology will form the topic of the next chapter.

3. Renewal of Moral Theology

Renewal of moral theology inevitably becomes associated with the popularized notion of "the New Morality," with all the unfortunate overtones this conveys. To the man on the street, this term has a sexual connotation and "the New Morality" implies "the New Sexuality." The sexual revolution, a more permissive atmosphere in the theater, cinema and literature, and the Playboy propaganda conjure up images of man in revolt against traditional mores. Mention of love as the only absolute value sounds similar to the drug-saturated hippie culture of love (luv). The New Morality threatens many; renewal in moral theology bears the same fate.

It has become commonplace to state that the New Morality is actually very old, for its basic inspiration stems from the healthy Gospel morality which became distorted and sick throughout the ages. Daniel C. Maguire writes in this vein: "The New Morality is also very old. It is just that the old seems new when rediscovered. Much in this case is as old as the Gospel of Jesus. Somehow or other, Christians have conspired to make the Good News seem bad. The Gospel comes across, especially to the young, as anti-fun, and many do not get much beyond that gloomy indictment. We have failed to communicate the news that Jesus challenged the world to try a new kind of love, a love that was more demanding, more electrifying and more humanizing than any ever known to man" ("The New Morality in Focus," in *Toward Moral Maturity,* ed. M. P. Ryan [Paramus, N.J.: Paulist Press, 1968], 5-21; cf. also O. Barr, *The Christian New Morality* [N.Y.: Oxford University Press, 1969], esp. 3-18).

No one can fault the basic thrust of this statement. But the catch-all phrase "the New Morality" may well imply for given authors far more than the rediscovery of Jesus' message about love. In the name of the New Morality and a truly evangelical morality, for example, Maguire opens the possibility of a morality of compromise, which permits exceptions to the ideal in such areas as abortion and divorce. To say that "all of this is basically old theology" seems misleading (Maguire, 5). A morality of compromise whereby ideals are accommodated to the concrete human condition may be a valid insight recapturing the Gospel, but it surely constitutes an enormous change from what is ordinarily meant by "old theology." (See C. Curran, *A New Look at Christian Morality* [Notre Dame: Fides, 1968] 16-21 for a brief explanation of a morality of compromise; also C. van Ouwerkerk, "Gospel Morality and Human Compromise," *Concilium* 5 [1965] 7-21.)

The renewal of moral theology advocated here will seem a far cry from the sensationalized versions of the New Morality. Its results will, it is hoped, not tend toward the laxism and hedonism decried by some protesters against the current mood in morals. It will strive instead to outline some principal features which should characterize Christian reflection on morals. A brief mention of the historical antecedents of the present-day renewal will serve as an introduction.

INITIATIVES TOWARD RENEWAL

J. Ford-G. Kelly, *Contemporary Moral Theology* (Paramus, N.J.: Newman, 1958) Vol. I, 61-73, outlines the views of Vermeersch, Schilling, Mersch and Tillmann.

R. Dailey, "New Approaches to Moral Theology," in *Current Trends in Theology,* ed. D. Wolf-J. Schall, 184-88, summarizes the themes of Tillmann, Gilleman and Häring.

A. Jonsen, *Responsibility in Modern Religious Ethics* (Washington: Corpus, 1968) 86-107, provides an excellent summation of Häring's thought on responsibility.

C. Curran, "The Moral Theology of Bernard Häring," in *A New Look at Christian Morality* (Notre Dame: Fides, 1968) 145-57, supplies a handy and readable summary.

Many initiatives toward the reformulation and updating of moral theology occurred between the two World Wars, mainly in Europe. Arthur Vermeersch, Otto Schilling, Emile Mersch, and Fritz Tillmann made notable contributions. The two works which have borne the most influence in recent years are G. Gilleman's *The Primacy of Charity in Moral Theology* and B. Häring's *The Law of Christ*. Through his lecture tours and frequent publications in English, Häring has exercised a great impact on the American scene in the past few years, though his books vary enormously in quality in every way. His central idea of response-responsibility has been his most influential stress.

In addition to these works, many articles have outlined general approaches toward renewal based on contemporary scriptural scholarship, theological and philosophical insights, and the social sciences. Enda McDonagh's words of several years ago nevertheless have a perduring validity: "These overdue developments are merely the beginning of what it is hoped will be a thorough gradual renewal of moral theology. . . . I should say that the development in moral theology was still in its infancy" ("Moral Theology Renewed," *Irish Ecclesiastical Record* 104 [1965] 321-32, at 321).

Many authors have attempted to organize their material around a central theme or motif, for example, the imitation of Christ (Tillmann), the mystical body (Mersch), the Kingdom of God (Stelzenberger), charity (Gilleman and, in special moral, Häring). Rather than discuss each author's contributions and viewpoint separately, we prefer to present an overview of these modern tendencies, all of which possess some scriptural basis, by incorporating them into our own presentation. Josef Fuchs estimates these efforts in the following way: "These attempts should be highly praised—as long as they avoid a sort of preaching. In such an approach, there can be imparted an integral and not merely moral (or 'moralistic') vision of man's life, flowing from the doctrine about the mystery of Christ and our salvation. It doesn't matter whether the principle of unity is also objectively the only true principle of moral theology" ("Theologia moralis perficienda," *Periodica* 55 [1966] 528).

ELEMENTS OF RENEWED MORAL THEOLOGY

The central mystery of revelation, the Trinity, should serve as the chief integrating element in renewed moral theology. Through their roles in the divine plan of salvation, the three Persons reveal themselves to man, and man's moral task should acknowledge the part played by each Person. The Father, ever loving and merciful to sinful man, initiates man's salvation and accomplishes it by sending his Son into the world "to unify all things under one head, Christ" (Eph. 1:10). By his saving actions, Jesus reconciles man and the world to the Father and extends this grace to each person by sending the Holy Spirit to the Church in his name. The Father thus manifests himself to man and realizes his plan of salvation through the Son; man responds to the Father in the Son through the power and the guidance of the Holy Spirit. This context, proper to all theological endeavor, recalls briefly that the new life in Christ involves man's cooperation with this activity of the three divine Persons in the whole world and in each person. A renewed moral theology must draw out the full implications of this trinitarian context.

One clear implication is that moral theology should follow the covenantal pattern of the Old Testament and the New Testament, that is, moral life should appear as a response to God's inviting Word. All men are called to be God's adopted sons by sharing his Spirit; in this lies salvation. "Like the Israelite of old, the Christian is to respond to the divine initiative with a response of love embodied in and validated by his worship and his conformity to God's will in his day-to-day living" (N. Crotty, "Biblical Perspectives in Moral Theology," *Theological Studies* 26 [1965] 574-95, at 578). Stress on this dialogical character of moral theology will result in a healthy personalism founded on God's revelation. God will not appear as the invisible Lawmaker or as the philosophers' Supreme Being, but rather as the God who loves man in creating, redeeming and sanctifying him. Moral life emerges as a meeting or encounter with God who speaks personal words. The focal point is God himself, not laws, or impersonal forces, or man. Moral norms may be explained as abstract expressions and summations of God's concrete calls for response in essentially similar situations. The Kantian emphasis on obedience to law will seem out of keeping with this personalistic approach. Likewise, the most enlightened self-seeking under the guise of perfectionism will be no substitute for God-seeking. Self-perfectionism may, in fact, imply a certain subordination of God to man's self-fulfillment. A moral theology which remains aware of the trinitarian background of all God's words will thus lay stress on man's present and future transforming union with God himself in three Persons. The Law, the works of the Law, and man's self-perfection will recede from the forefront of the moral life. God himself in three Persons will be the term of man's dialogue.

God issues his invitation to man in and through Christ, and man responds only in, with and through Christ. "No one can come to the Father except through me. If you know me, you know my Father too" (John 14:6). This divine self-manifestation in Christ, God speaking to man and man in total response to God, should dominate the themes of moral theology. The fact that God has become incarnate and assumed man's condition in all but sin should influence the whole of Christian living: Christ himself becomes the moral norm; natural law has a Christological foundation; salvation is not far off, but already achieved, and man's moral life applies these mysteries to the individual Christian; unity in Christ alone adequately fulfills God's revealed designs for man.

The Christian's efforts to live in Christ will lead him to seek out the vital sources in which he continues to reveal himself: the Church, the written Word of Sacred Scripture, and the sacraments, particularly the Eucharist. The Word of God in the Bible reveals the gradual self-disclosure of God to man and lends "the principal witness of the life and teaching of the Incarnate Word, our Savior" (*Dogmatic Constitution on Divine Revelation,* n. 18). The sacraments form the high points of Jesus' communicating himself to the responsive Christian. Attention to this sacramental dimension of man's activity will permit moral theology to penetrate more the gratuitous character of Christian living as a real gift from God, to stress the worshiping aspect of every human project, and to indicate the value of the Christian's life as a witness before men of Christ's life in him. The Eucharistic liturgy will be viewed as the summit of this intense life and the foremost sign and source of life in Christ. These developments will provide an antidote to some unhealthy tendencies noted in Catholic presentations of morality, which have struck some as being insufficiently related to the message of salvation announced in Jesus.

The biblical teaching on conversion (metanoia) should animate treatments of man's response to God. Jesus preached the need of a continual conversion (literally, a turnabout) through personal and growing commitment to the Father through the Son. Moral theology tended in recent times to conceive the moral life as a series of individual acts which are termed virtuous or sinful. Recovery of the biblical notion of conversion will lead to an emphasis on the totality of man's posture before God rather than on his individual choices. (See R. Schnackenburg, *Christian Existence in the New Testament,* Vol. 1, 33-66.) These latter options will be viewed within the broader context of the person's basic option or life-orientation to or away from God and will be considered to take their full moral significance only within this perspective. This biblically inspired approach seems more consonant too with the insights of contemporary psychology, which stresses the entire process of self-realization instead of single acts. One happy result will be the dynamism this approach brings to moral theology, for a Christian will be seen as either going forward, however gradually, toward God or backward away from him, into sinfulness. "Staying out of sin" or "not breaking the law" ignores this movement and distorts the Christian proclamation of the merciful Father who calls in Christ and to whom man comes a step at a time. (See R. McCormick, "The Moral Theology of Vatican II," in *The Future of Ethics and Moral Theology* [Argus Communication Co., 1968] 7-18; R. O'Neil-M. Donovan, *Sexuality and Moral Responsibility* [Washington: Corpus Books, 1968], chap. II; J. Fuchs, *Human Values and Christian Morality,* 92-111.)

Insights gained from Sacred Scripture will lead also to an ecclesial and social morality. Salvation history indicates that God has chosen a people to himself and calls the individual within community. Man's personal response to God never occurs apart from community and man cannot ignore this corporate dimension of his moral life. The commitment to community which results from birth and baptism cannot be set aside as a matter of free decision. A self-centered, individualistic morality does not agree with Jesus' preaching of morality as loving service of one's neighbor. Morality must respect the social nature of man and treat the relevant social issues which affect people today. Race, poverty, and war—the great social issues of the day—must enter more fully into the Christian's consciousness as grave moral concerns. Ethical problems in advertising, middle management positions, housing, technology, aid to underdeveloped peoples and overpopulation must complement traditional discussions of justice, which favored an overly individualistic understanding of the new life in Christ.

Renewed moral theology should, moreover, mirror the positive qualities of the Gospel message, the Good News of salvation in Christ. The resurrection of Jesus means that sin has already been conquered and that a new, joyful life awaits the believer. Why then concentrate on sin and its avoidance? God does not invite man to no-thing, to not-do things, to avoid things. He invites man to love him and one's fellow men. The moral values of justice, truth, or chastity inherent in concrete situations should be seen as opportunities to love God, to whom one responds in seeking the value. Universal negative prohibitions (for example, against adultery) should be presented as formulations protecting an underlying positive value. The legitimate contributions of modern value-philosophy about moral realities as the fulfillment of human exigencies and strivings can prove a fine asset in this renewal of moral theology.

Finally, the day has passed when theological reflection relied solely on Catholic sources. A renewed theology of the life in Christ must draw on the full breadth of Christian tradition in the Churches and be ecumenically oriented. This process has already begun to some extent, especially in the present-day Catholic controversies about absolute norms in moral theology, which have utilized Protestant writings on contextualism and situation ethics. (E. Outka-P. Ramsey, *Norm and Context in Christian Ethics*, is a fine example of ecumenical collaboration on this basic issue.)

BIBLIOGRAPHY

Böckle, F., *Fundamental Concepts of Moral Theology* (Paramus, N.J.: Paulist Press, 1968).

Conway, W., "The Science of Moral: New Trends," *Irish Theological Quarterly* 22 (1955) 154-58.

Crotty, N., "Biblical Perspectives in Moral Theology," *Theological Studies* 269 (1965) 574-96.

Curran, C., *A New Look at Christian Morality* (Notre Dame: Fides, 1968).

Dailey, R., "New Approaches to Moral Theology," in *Current Trends in Moral Theology*, ed. D. Wolf-J. Schall (Garden City: Image Books, 1966) 162-89.

Doyle, J., "New Perspectives in Moral Theology," *Homiletic & Pastoral Review* 63 (1963) 385-91.

Dwyer, R., "Moral Theology: New Horizons in Contemporary Moral Theology," *Critic* 21 (1962) 31-35.

Ford, J.-Kelly, G., *Contemporary Moral Theology*, Vol. I (Paramus, N.J.: Newman, 1958) chap. 4-6.

Fuchs, J., *Human Values and Christian Morality,* (Dublin: Gill and Macmillan, 1970).

Gilleman, G.: "Moral Theology and Charity," *Theology Digest* 2 (1954) 15-18.

————, *The Primacy of Charity in Moral Theology* (Paramus, N.J.: Newman, 1959).

Häring, B., "The Dynamism of Christian Life," *Chicago Studies* 4 (1965) 253-73.

————, *The Law of Christ*, 3 vols. (Paramus, N.J.: Newman, 1961, 1963, 1966); Vol. I, 3-33.

————, "Moral Theology and the Apostolic Formation of the Priest," in *Apostolic Renewal in the Seminary* (N.Y.: The Christophers, 1965) 174-84.

————, "Moral Theology. Catholic," *Sacramentum Mundi*, Vol. IV (N.Y.: Herder & Herder, 1969) 122-28.

Healy, G., "Recent Moral Theology," *Philippine Studies* 9 (1961) 311-32.

Leonard, J., "Criticisms and Problems of Modern Moral Theology," *American Ecclesiastical Review* 145 (1961) 331-37.

McCormick, R., "The Primacy of Charity," *Perspectives* (1959) 18-27.

McDonagh, E., "Moral Theology Today," *Irish Theological Quarterly* 28 (1961) 299-303.

————, "Moral Theology: The Need for Renewal," *Irish Theological Quarterly* 31 (1964) 269-82.

————, "Moral Theology Renewed," *Irish Ecclesiastical Record* 104 (1965) 321-32.

————, "Teaching Moral Theology Today," *Irish Theological Quarterly* 33 (1966) 195-207.

Milhaven, J., *Toward A New Catholic Morality* (Garden City, N.Y.: Doubleday, 1970).

Murnion, P., "The Renewal of Moral Theology: Review and Prospect," *Dunwoodie Review* 3 (1963) 39-65.

Pinckaers, S., "Revival of Moral Theology," *Cross Currents* 7 (1957) 56-67.

Rahner, K., *Nature and Grace* (N.Y.: Sheed & Ward, 1964).

————, *The Dynamic Element in the Church* (N.Y.: Herder & Herder, 1964).

Schnackenburg, R., *The Moral Teaching of the New Testament* (N.Y.: Herder & Herder, 1965).

Spicq, C., *The Trinity and Our Moral Life According to St. Paul.* (Paramus, N.J.: Newman, 1963). Published in Great Britain under the title *St. Paul and Christian Living* (Dublin: Gill and Son, 1964).

Stevens, G., "Current Trends in Moral Theology," *Catholic Educational Review* 58 (1960) 1-11.

Thomas, A., "Progress and Prospects in Moral Theology," *Nat. Cath. Educ. Assoc. Bulletin 60* (1963) 51-59.

van der Marck, W., *Toward a Christian Ethic* (Paramus, N.J.: Newman, 1967).

Voll, U., "Contemporary Developments in Sacramental and

Moral Theology," Society of Cath. Coll. Teachers of Christian Doct. *Proceedings* 8 (1962) 122-37.

————, "The Present State of Christian Moral Teaching," Society of Cath. Coll. Teachers of Christian Doct. *Proceedings* 9 (1963) 10-20.

4. Sons in the Son

God's fatherhood and our sonship occupy a central position in the New Testament. St. John sees this filial relation as the goal of God's intervention into human history in the incarnation: "Think of the love that the Father has lavished on us, by letting us be called God's children; and that is what we are. . . . We are already the children of God, but what we are to be in the future has not yet been revealed; all we know is that when it is revealed we shall be like him because we shall see him as he really is" (1 John 3:1-2). St. Paul writes in a similar vein that we have become "sons of God by adoption" and "new creatures according to God" (cf. Eph. 1:3-6; 2 Cor. 5:17).

God the Father invites us to be his sons and the Holy Spirit confers this sonship. This gives us a sharing in the very life of the glorified Christ, allowing us to participate in the divine nature according to his pattern. The Father foreknew and predestined all the chosen to be "images of his Son" (Rom. 8:29). This sonship is not a merely legal adoption or some form of extrinsic bond. The new man shares by baptism in the special relationship that unites Christ with the Father. This new being not only determines man's present relationship of sonship with the Father, but also provides the basic standard for the moral imperative of the Christian: "You must therefore be perfect just as your heavenly Father is perfect" (Matt. 5:48). (See Schnackenburg, *Christian Existence in the New Testament,* Vol. I, 158-89.)

Jesus' full sharing in our human nature and our union with the Risen Lord form the basis of our sonship. He has a primacy over all creation: "All things were created through him and for him. Before anything was created, he existed, and he holds all things in unity. Now the Church is his body, he is her head. As he is the beginning, he was first to be born from the dead, so that he should be first in every way, because God wanted all perfection to be found in him and all things to be reconciled through him and for him" (Col. 1:16-20). This sharing in our nature differs in its roots from the closest union or identification of one human being with another, for example, the union into one flesh of husband and wife, or the union of parents and children. The fullest identification of Jesus with his disciples, both as a group and individually, emerges clearly in his preaching. "On that day you will understand that I am in my Father and you in me and I in you" (John 14:20). Sharing in Christ's life is likened to the union of the vine and its branches, signifying the mutual interpenetration between Jesus and believers (John 15:4-8). "From his fullness we have all received" (John 1:16). This is the mysterious dynamism of the Christian life, calling for cooperation of the Christian, and typified in the Eucharistic communion: "He who eats my flesh and drinks my blood lives in me and I live in him" (John 6:56-57).

Reflecting on this teaching, St. Paul views it as the fundamental experience and basis of Christian existence. As sons of God, as "members of his body" (Eph. 4:15), all Christians are called by God as "co-heirs with Christ" (Rom. 8:17; Gal. 4:6). "To live in Christ" becomes the concrete moral norm for the Christian. The phrases which occur more than one hundred and sixty times with such insistence—in Christ Jesus, in Christ, in the Lord—all signify a union with the glorified Christ. This union is so real that "for anyone who is in Christ, there is a new creation; the old creation has gone, and now the new one is here" (2 Cor. 5:17). Through baptism, the Christian dies to sin, to the carnal man, and is no longer under the Law (Rom. 6:1-11). The new man in Christ is justified, spiritual, a servant of justice, and possesses the Spirit of Christ, who vivifies and moves him (Rom. 6:14-18; 8:2, 14-16). As all the members of the human body, though they are many, form one body, so all Christians are united in Christ (1 Cor. 12:12). From Christ "the whole body, supplied and built up by joints and ligaments, attains a growth that is of God" (Col. 2:19). So close is this union of all believers with Christ and with one another that "if one member suffers anything, all the members suffer it too, and if one member is honored, all the members rejoice together" (1 Cor. 12:26).

As sons of God, we are summoned to reach out beyond ourselves in love, to open ourselves to the cleansing action of the
Holy Spirit. Borne on by this Spirit of Jesus, the adopted son will
lead a dynamic life of moral growth, tending always toward the
ideal proposed in Christ. "If we live by the truth and in love, we
shall grow in all ways into Christ, who is the head by whom the
whole body is fitted and joined together, every joint adding its
own strength, for each separate part to work according to its
function. So the body grows until it has built itself up in love"
(Eph. 4:15-16). "Even though our union with Christ has been
effected by baptism, this union can grow. By baptism we have
become God's children and we have been conformed to the image
of his Son. . . . But this likeness can increase. Our life in
Christ is therefore at the same time a fact and a demand, and the
fact includes the demand" (G. Bouwman, *The Bible on the
Imitation of Christ,* 86). This life will certainly not, therefore,
violate the Father's will, for the love of a son in the Son is proved
by his radical obedience: "Anybody who receives my Commandments and keeps them will be one who loves me; and anybody who loves me will be loved by my Father, and I shall love
him and show myself to him" (John 14:21).

God's Word in Sacred Scripture expresses this moral demand
based on our factual union in Christ in two main ways: the
following of Christ and the imitation of Christ. Though closely
related, these concepts remain distinct. The former stresses personal adherence to and communion with Jesus as disciples, and
the latter emphasizes the example given by Christ to his followers.
Following Christ as a disciple actually includes all aspects of living
in Christ. (Besides Bouwman, see also K. Schelkle, *Discipleship
and Priesthood,* 9-32, R. Schnackenburg, *The Moral Teaching of
the New Testament,* 42-53, and *id.,* "The Imitation of Christ," in
Christian Existence in the New Testament, Vol. 1, 99-127.)

FOLLOWING CHRIST

Jesus spoke frequently of following him, as when he called
Simon and Andrew: "Follow me and I will make you into fishers
of men. And at once they left their nets and followed him"

(Mark 1:17-18). "To follow" or "to go after" is the characteristic biblical expression for "to become someone's disciple." This invitation of Jesus was directed not only to the small group of apostles, but to others whom he calls to discipleship (e.g., the rich young man in Mark 10:17-22). Jesus thus invites these chosen disciples to share his life and mission, to enter into a living and personal relationship with him during his historical undertaking. The physical coming to Jesus or accompanying him must result in something deeper than this, a following in the spiritual sense. "In all the places where the expression 'to follow' is found in the New Testament—seventy-eight times—there is question of following a person, and this person is, with a single exception (Mark 14:13), always Christ. Moreover, the word is restricted to the Gospels, where following Christ in his earthly life is always indicated" (Bouwman, 24-25; actually the word is also used in Apoc. 14:4).

Jesus' disciples were to share not only his friendship ("I call you friends," John 15:15), but his destiny as well, including hatred, suffering, persecution, and death: "You will be hated by all men on account of my name; but the man who stands firm to the end will be saved . . . . The disciple is not superior to his teacher, nor the slave to his master" (Matt. 10:22, 24). "Because you do not belong to the world, because my choice withdrew you from the world, therefore, the world hates you. Remember the words I said to you: A servant is not greater than his master. If they persecuted me, they will persecute you too" (John 15:19-20). Jesus repeatedly made strong demands on those whom he called: they had to leave everything, family, house, and farm, money and wealth, their former occupations, and economic security. The filial duty of burying one's own father must take second place to the preaching of the Kingdom (Luke 9:59-62), and his disciples must love him more than father, mother, children, sisters, brothers, or even their own lives (Luke 14:26; see Bouwman, 40).

In its original meaning, "following Christ" applies only to communion with the historical Christ. "The reason is that this term is always limited to expressing a relationship which is continuing and actually taking place and which is not present except in its very discharge—a relationship, therefore, to the Lord in his visible presence, in his contemporaneousness, in his historical reality.

The spiritual relationship of the faithful to the exalted Christ and Lord is not described in this way" (Schelkle, 25-26). This usage of "following Christ" appears without exception in the Synoptic Gospels and the term is employed outside the Gospels only in Apocalypse 14:4. In the Gospel of John, however, "following Christ" means more than in the Synoptics. "To follow Christ means to believe in his Word, to keep his commands, especially his command of love in a trusting surrender. Whoever follows him in this way enters upon a communion of life with the glorified Lord, a communion which is infinitely more intimate than the purely corporeal nearness of the Master to his disciples" (Bouwman, 36-37; see R. Schnackenburg, *Christian Existence in the New Testament,* Vol. 1, 114f.).

Contemporary Christians may gain insight into the unconditional and irrevocable commitment to Christ demanded of them from these biblical notions. Wholehearted adherence to and communion with Christ is offered and expected of the faithful disciple of today. The call to follow, nevertheless, remains God's free gift, a grace: "No one can come to me unless the Father allows him" (John 6:65).

IMITATING CHRIST

Jesus explicitly cites himself on several occasions as an historical example whom his followers should imitate. After washing his apostles' feet, he proposes his spirit of service for their imitation: "If I, then, the Lord and Master, have washed your feet, you should wash each other's feet. I have given you an example so that you may copy what I have done to you" (John 13:14-15). He also refers his disciples to his love: "I give you a new commandment: love one another; just as I have loved you, you also must love one another" (John 13:34). St. John draws the full moral conclusion: "We can be sure that we are in God only when the one who claims to be living in him is living the same kind of life as Christ lived" (1 John 2:5-6). St. Peter also proposes Christ as a model, for by his passion he "suffered for you and left an example for you to follow the way he took" (1 Peter 2:21). In all these examples, imitating Christ does not mean merely to copy him, but to follow him as a model. The richer concept of following Christ thus implies imitating him.

St. Paul repeatedly introduces the theme of imitating Christ and succinctly summarizes the doctrine: "Take me for your model, as I take Christ" (1 Cor. 11:1). Baptism confers a likeness to Christ and plunges us into the life and death of Jesus. The Christian task is to live out this God-given, sacramental likeness: "You have been taught that when we were baptized in Christ Jesus we were baptized in his death; in other words, when we were baptized we went into the tomb with him and joined him in death, so that as Christ was raised from the dead by the Father's glory, we too might live a new life. If in union with Christ we have imitated his death, we shall also imitate him in his resurrection" (Rom. 6:3-5). We are to imitate in action the Christ to whom we are assimilated in our mystical union through baptism. "Practically, one can say that Paul reduces Christian ethics to the imitation of Christ" (Bouwman, 71). Yet Paul's notion of imitation has a special note: "Paul very seldom points to the example that Christ gave during the days of his earthly life; his idea is not to imitate as exactly as possible the historical life of Jesus. Paul himself had been called by the glorified Kyrios; it is to him that he looks. The great mysteries of the incarnation, the death and the resurrection of the Lord are for him the norm and the motive for the Christian life" (Bouwman, 75). In contemporary terminology, one would say that Paul has an ontological understanding of imitating Christ based on our union with him in baptism.

Sacred Scripture thus shows the validity of recourse to the notion of imitating Christ. And yet, what does imitating Christ imply? Does this mean mimicry of his external actions, an actual repetition of his words and deeds? This would be obviously impossible, though some trends in the past tended in this direction. Distorted tendencies in spirituality over the centuries have in fact given a somewhat pejorative meaning to the notion of imitating Christ. Luther and many Protestants after him reacted to an outlook which lent credence to man's capacity to act like Christ. Man cannot imitate Christ on his own; God's gift precedes his summons. We do not become children of our heavenly

Father by imitating Christ; rather, being children of God we should endeavor to live as true sons. Contemporary theology balances these valid insights, which lay stress on God's sovereign grace, with a recognition of the real expectancy of human cooperation: God's call is at once a gift and a demand.

Rightly understood, imitation of Christ means the gradual acquiring of and conformity to the mind and attitudes of Christ. Through personal familiarity with Christ, a Christian learns to react in a Christ-like manner in his own situation and according to his native capacities. Grace operates throughout this entire life-enterprise. "The important thing is that we relinquish our own purely human evaluation and conform ourselves to his mind and live our life according to his scale of values. Without this, all exterior imitation is only mimicry and a pose. And not only this: it is also contrary to Christian liberty, which enjoins us to develop our personality according to this new scale of values to the full stature of Christ (Eph. 4:13). Purely exterior imitation has value only if it is an expression of love, and expression of the desire to enter into a union with Christ which is as intimate as possible: to be where he is" (Bouwman, 67-68).

Imitation of any model presupposes thorough comprehension of the model and an admiration borne out in personal living. In seeking out this model, one can turn to Sacred Scripture, where believers can "learn by frequent reading . . . the 'excelling knowledge of Jesus Christ' (Phil. 3:8). 'For ignorance of the Scriptures is ignorance of Christ' (St. Jerome). Therefore, they should gladly put themselves in touch with the sacred text itself, whether it be through the liturgy, rich in the divine Word, or through devotional reading, or through instructions suitable for the purpose and other aids which, in our time, are commendably available everywhere" (*Dogmatic Constitution on Divine Revelation*, n. 25).

Imitation of Jesus will permit Christians to rise above many difficulties and sufferings by faith in the Father, who bears in his hands the reins of human destiny. Jesus did not sidestep miseries inherent in human existence, but faced them squarely, strengthened by trust in his Father. His life was consumed in loving service of men for the love of the Father; this was the content of his daily labors, of his way of the cross, and of his death on the cross. In patterning his life according to this model, a Christian believer expresses in his own life Jesus' self-description: "Anyone who wants to be great among you must be your servant, and anyone who wants to be first among you must be your slave, just as the Son of Man came not to be served but to serve, and to give his life as a ransom for many" (Matt. 20:26-28). (R. Schnackenburg, *Christian Existence in the New Testament,* Vol. 1, 122-27, makes concrete application of the biblical notions to the Christian situation today.)

A Present Reality and Pledge of the Future

The Kingdom of God has broken into human history in the coming of Jesus, though it remains incomplete. The present offering of eternal life as sons in the Son serves as a pledge of that life of full sonship which believers will share in the Kingdom of the Father. Sacramental union with Christ in baptism already implies that the believer "has eternal life. . . . He has passed from death to life" (John 5:24). Personal communion with Christ means that the promised Kingdom has further transformed the believer. Eternal life is not merely a future, ultimate state, but begins here and now as a present, but partial and precarious, reality. Real Christian life begins on earth, not in heaven. (See F. Bourdeau-A. Danet, *Introduction to the Law of Christ* [N.Y.: Alba House, 1966] 91-92.)

Life in Christ thus has the dual aspect of a present and future reality, of partial fulfillment and continuing expectancy of completion. No discontinuity exists between the present and the future, for the eschatological Kingdom becomes present already in the person, words and deeds of Christ. "To come to the Kingdom means to come to Jesus, this and no more, that is to say, it means to be a disciple who harkens to his Gospel" (E. Thurneysen, *The Sermon on the Mount* [Richmond: John Knox, 1964] 34). The believer is united now to Christ as the Father's adopted son; he shares in the Kingdom of God and enjoys communion with the Father in Christ; he has been conformed to the image of Christ the High Priest. The final coming of the Kingdom will complete, perfect and make permanent this present sonship. God will fully and permanently offer himself face to face, giving us our glorification with the glorified Lord: "For us, our home is in heaven, and from heaven comes the Savior we are waiting for, the Lord Jesus Christ, and he will transfigure these wretched bodies of ours into copies of his glorious body. . . . So then, my brothers and dear friends, do not give way but remain faithful in the Lord" (Phil. 3:20–4:1).

Jesus conveys a sense of urgency connected with this coming of the Kingdom. God's reign has begun and is hastening to its conclusion: "The time has come . . . and the Kingdom of God is close at hand. Repent, and believe the Good News" (Mark 1:15). The presence of the Kingdom makes an absolute, unconditional, and radical claim on his followers. The Father's offer of love cannot be refused; his call demands a response. Nothing matters more than faith in Jesus and obedience to the Father, leading to loving service of the neighbor in need. Only those who now accept and live out this message of Jesus will one day hear him say: "Come, you whom my Father has blessed, take for your heritage the Kingdom prepared for you since the foundation of the world" (Matt. 25:34). Jesus thereby proclaims that the future faces man in the present and requires of him a decision for God or for the world. Love of the neighbor in need constitutes the prime requisite for openness to God's future. G. Moran summarizes well the preceding: "Man's entrance into final communion is at once the realization of the perfection of man and the glorification of God. Man discovers that he becomes himself in his union with the Son and as adopted son. The total receptivity demanded of a son is the way in which the creature 'gives glory.' It is not by offering external objects that he glorifies God, but by living the life of a son in union with all mankind: 'The glory of God is man fully alive' (Irenaeus)" (*Theology of Revelation*, 188).

The tension between present, partial salvation through life in Christ and future, complete salvation provides a fertile source of moral obligation for the Christian. The new life of sonship and the offer of the Kingdom do not remain on the ontological, static level, as "givens." Man possesses mastery of his life-project of self-realization in Christ through his free response to God's gift. "The reign of God is present but not fully present. The incipient presence of the eschaton calls for a continual growth and development. The followers of Jesus can never rest content with the present" (C. Curran, *A New Look at Christian Morality*, 13; see R. Schnackenburg, *The Moral Teaching of the New Testament*, 15-25; T. Oden, *Radical Obedience. The Ethics of Rudolph Bultmann* [Philadelphia: Westminster, 1964], 25-45).

Man's present life emerges as a task and a challenge in this biblical perspective. A restlessness and dissatisfaction with past achievements and a desire for deeper fidelity to God's graces should characterize a Christian faithful to Christ's message. His time, space, and activities allow him to unfold the implications of his baptismal sonship. The present hour, the moment at hand assumes major importance, for it embodies God's call. God's own love creates in him the desire to continue the divine creative work on earth. Temporal tasks take on an intrinsic worth and contribute to the Christian's existence of sharing God's own glory in union with Christ. Man's unfolding in history cannot be viewed as irrelevant or incidental to his final fulfillment in the eschatological Kingdom.

Sanctifying Grace and the Beatific Vision

The theological expression of this scriptural teaching on divine sonship and union with Christ occurs in connection with the doctrine of sanctifying grace. The basic insight that God offers himself in personal love to each man and shares his life with him as a son lies at the root of this theology. God, who alone is holy, sanctifies man by creating in him the capacity to receive and cooperate with his grace given in sovereign freedom. Man's powers are elevated through the very self-communication of God. "God, who probes the heart, awaits him there. There he discerns his proper destiny beneath the eyes of God" (*Pastoral Constitution on the Church in the Modern World*, n. 14).

Sacred Scripture attributes this divine action of grace to the Holy

Spirit, who molds us into the image of Christ. The new life in Christ is, then, a life in response to the movement of the Holy Spirit. To be in sanctifying grace means that the genuine Christian acts "according to the Spirit" (Rom. 8:4; Gal. 5:18). The Spirit alone leads the Christian to a full conviction of sonship in Christ: "Everyone moved by the Spirit is a son of God. The spirit you received is not the spirit of slaves bringing fear into your lives again; it is the spirit of sons, and it makes us cry out, 'Abba, Father!' The Spirit himself and our spirit bear united witness that we are children of God. And if we are children we are heirs as well: heirs of God and co-heirs with Christ, sharing his sufferings so as to share his glory" (Rom. 8:14-17; cf. Gal. 4:6-7). (See C. Spicq, *The Trinity and Our Moral Life According to St. Paul,* chap. IV.)

Only the sons of God, made such through sanctifying grace, will attain the complete eternal life offered in Christ. Though grace is a gratuitous gift of God, its bestowal presupposes sufficient dispositions and cooperation on the part of an adult. God does not view man as a totally passive recipient of his favors. Perseverance in responsiveness to the Spirit likewise requires a moral and religious willingness in each person. Though the grace of the Spirit is always sufficiently offered, the living faith of a Christian serves in God's plan as a true cause meriting a present increase of grace and the future realization of eternal life.

This offering of God's friendship in sanctifying grace and its completion in the beatific vision is not, finally, a mere possibility, one choice among many others, held out for man's acceptation or rejection. No person, even the pagan, can fall back upon a "natural morality" or a "natural end" if he fails to live the unique life of the Spirit. No union with God has existed or does exist other than sanctifying grace and the beatific vision. The task of believer and non-believer alike is to assume as his personal life-project the present and future attainment of that life offered in Christ. Just how the non-believer, especially the atheist, unites himself to Christ, the unique Way to salvation, remains the object of intense theological speculation and discussion. That every person finds salvation by responding to the Father as a son in the Son through the power of the Holy Spirit forms the starting point for this

Christian reflection. (See P. Fransen, "How Can Non-Christians Find Salvation in Their Own Religions?" in *Christian Revelation and World Religions,* ed. J. Neuner [London: Burns & Oates, 1967] 67-122; J. Fuchs, *Human Values and Christian Morality,* 13-15, 68-70.)

Life in Christ for the Father

One conclusion follows from the preceding: our present and future union with the glorious Christ, the God-man, is the real goal which gives meaning to the Christian's life. All things have been created through him and with him, and the world is "his own" (John 1:11-12). The Christian can do no other thing than reascend to the Father in, through and with Christ: "For us there is one God, the Father, from whom all things come and through whom we exist" (1 Cor. 8:6). The scale of values always ascends from the Christian through Christ to the Father: "The world, life and death, the present and the future, are all your servants; but you belong to Christ and Christ belongs to God" (1 Cor. 3:22-23). Christian life must model itself on the mystery of Christ's own divine sonship and of his humanity, by which he is less than the Father (John 14:28) and is sent as the Way to the Father. In pondering this sonship of Jesus, we see that the Father sent him, redeemed the world through him, raised him from the dead and set him in glory on his right hand, made all creation subject to him, waiting for the consummation when the Son with his Kingdom would submit to the Father. "In a humanity which is like to ours in all respects, save sin, he is constituted leader not only over the Church of the redeemed, but over the world as well. He is filled, from God, with all the energy and perfection corresponding to this mission. . . . Jesus himself has opened and wholly offered his consciousness, his soul, his understanding, his will, his heart, and finally his body, so as to be perfectly what God wanted him to be, namely, the minister and leader of the world's salvation" (Y. Congar, *Jesus Christ* [N.Y.: Herder & Herder]150-51).

A Christ-centered morality leads then ultimately to a Father-centered morality. We should live according to the pattern of Christ, the Son of God, "and when everything is subjected to him, then the Son himself will be subject in his turn to the One who subjected all things to him, so that God may be all in all" (1 Cor. 15:28). The Christian will live "for God in Christ Jesus" (Rom. 6:11), giving glory by doing his will (John 17:4) and striving to be perfect as the Father is perfect (Matt. 5:48). Assimilation to Christ means assimilation to the Father, of whom Christ is the image. "God reveals himself in man in order to bring him to adore what no eye has seen. God sends his Son to express the Father in human guise. We hear the Father in his human echo; in a human obedience to death we come to experience who it is that commands it; in the answer we have the Word. The Son as man, at the summit of the cosmos, executes before the Father the ecclesiastic, the cosmic liturgy. In him are joined Word and liturgy" (H. von Balthasar, *Word and Revelation* [N.Y.: Herder & Herder, 1964] 118).

Christian morality is, therefore, God-centered. This theocentrism is made more concrete in the person of God's Son, Jesus Christ. The Christian serves not merely the one God and Creator; assumed into a true trinitarian life, he serves the Father as a son in the Son by the power of the Holy Spirit. The newness of life in Christ is not, then, something simply added to our natural life. Rather, from their very selves, created anew in Christ Jesus, believers strive to offer filial service to the Father by way of Christ. They aim at a greater knowledge of him (Eph. 4:13; Phil. 3:10), in order to be transformed into him. "In this way we are all to come to unity in our faith and in our knowledge of the Son of God, until we become the perfect man, fully mature with the fullness of Christ himself" (Eph. 4:13).

CHRIST THE STANDARD OF CHRISTIAN MORALITY

Jesus' central role in creation and redemption forms the ultimate basis for the foregoing notions about sonship in him, following him, and imitating him. Christ effectively brings about the full design of God, not only in regard to his people, but also in regard to all creation. In creating the world, God already saw it in Christ. The eternal Word entered human history in the fullest way, becoming man and redeeming sinful man. In Jesus, the gift of the divine Word to man in his very divinity, God's invitation to man is fully and finally revealed. In the total response of the man who was God, man's response to this invitation is charted. Christ sums up in his person the invitation and response in a way that makes him the new covenant and the new moral norm. Through him and by being conformed to his image, men are truly men and share the new life offered by the Father. Christian response in any particular situation should be ultimately patterned on the original picture of the person of Christ, our archetype and example. E. McDonagh can say: "It is not what Christ explicitly taught, not any recorded ethical teaching of his that makes him the center of moral theology. It is what he was and is—God communicating himself in the fullest possible way to man, man responding in the fullest possible way to God. . . . Christ is the norm or standard by which moral behavior is now measured. He is the moral law" ("Moral Theology Renewed," *Irish Ecclesiastical Record* 104 [1965] 321-32, at 323).

In Christ, the moral order willed by God is made concrete, for he is a single person in whom the fullness of the world's salvation dwells. He is also the universal moral norm, for all reality is rooted in him and he is the measure of life for all. Even the so-called universal moral norms apply only because they have their basis in Christ, the ultimate pattern of all reality. Every truly human value, moreover, embodies the Christ-life, for all goodness is ultimately grounded in him. H. von Balthasar states this doctrine well: "In Jesus, a man unique and aware of his uniqueness, the Word of God reached men. God's Word is no longer an abstract law, it is this man. Everything God has to say or give to the world has found a place in him. The whole objective spirit of religion, of law, of ritual is identical with the subjective spirit of this particular man, a man like us. It is the religion of freedom. When this man gives God his all, obeys him to death, he obeys but himself, his love as Son for the Father. With him it is no longer any question of heteronomy or autonomy; the 'heteros,' the Father, is also 'to auton,' the same concrete nature. He who believes in the Son is free, for he has attained the true, absolute humanism" (*Word and Revelation,* 119; see also J. Fuchs, *Natural Law, A Theological Investigation* [N.Y.: Sheed & Ward, 1965] 73-84, and *id.,* "The Law of Christ," in *Human Values and Christian Morality,* 76-91).

COMMUNICATION WITH CHRIST

The glorified Christ shares his life and communicates with his followers through his grace offered in the Church and the sacraments. The primary divine gift is Uncreated Grace, God himself. When he offers himself to us, he realizes in us an interior transformation opening us to himself. "Grace is therefore not a 'thing,' a non-personal power that separates itself from God in order to take effect in man. Grace is God himself insofar as he communicates himself to man; and grace is man insofar as he is penetrated in a sanctifying way by God and thus achieves new being. Grace is in a proper sense a divine and human reality, the image of and participation in the incarnation of God in Jesus Christ" (O. Semmelroth, "The Christ-Event and Our Salvation," in *Man Before God* [N.Y.: P. J. Kenedy & Sons, 1966] 209-26, at 219-20). Grace thus brings Christ into contact with man, giving him a new life and thus making the moral law a more personal and internal reality. The grace of "the spirit of the life in Christ Jesus" (Rom. 8:2) serves as the prime guidance for the Christian, enlightening him and moving him to act in accord with his new sharing in Christ.

Through his earthly sign, the Church, Christ makes manifest his redeeming presence among men. The Church is herself the sacramental Christ, "the sign raised up among the nations" (Vatican I), Christ's salvation visibly realized in this world, "the Kingdom of God now present in mystery" (*Dogmatic Constitution on the Church,* n. 3). In viewing this visible communion in the grace of Christ, the Christian encounters the image of the Father revealed in the sign of the Christian community. In this body, "the life of Christ is poured into the believers, who, through the sacraments, are united in a hidden and real way to Christ who suffered and was glorified" (*ibid.*, n. 7). "The ecclesial body of Christ is established on earth by means of bodily mediations which put our bodies, that is, our whole persons, into contact with the paschal body of Jesus Christ" (Y. Congar, *Jesus Christ,* 152). Each sacrament is the personal saving act of the risen Christ, realized in the visible form of an official act of the Church. Christ himself, the eternally actual mystery of worship and salvation, becomes present to man in these ecclesial actions: "Christ baptizes . . . absolves, offers sacrifice" (*Mediator Dei*). Christ's divine love for men through his gift of interior grace takes visible form, and his human love for God through his worship becomes manifest. To receive a sacrament fruitfully, then, is to enter into the Church's communion of life with the risen Lord.

The Christian doctrine about entry into the Kingdom of heaven as sons of God in Christ finds its realization in the sacramental economy. In its own way, each sacrament draws men into the reality of Christ's death and resurrection. Through the sacraments we enter into immediate contact with the living Christ, the norm and center of our moral life; we become sons of God; we live in Christ; we share now in his Kingdom and long for its final realization and strive for it as pilgrims. St. Paul's teaching about our baptismal joining to Christ is verified also in the other sacraments. Confirmation strengthens our initial baptismal configuration to the crucified and glorified Christ by the fuller gift of the Spirit, impelling us to a deeper and more demanding adult Christian life in the service of others. The Eucharist, the continually renewed and personal sacramental union with Christ, repeatedly establishes and intensifies our new life in Christ. In Eucharistic celebration and communion all men are united in Christ their brother in his going to the Father. Penance renews or establishes in us the Christ who suffered for sinners, so that as penitents and converted sinners we may share the life of Christ and live for the Father. In the sacrament of the sick, Christ offers us a sharing in his life under the aspect of his sufferings, whereby he expressed his subjection to the will of the Father and his hope for definitive life with him. Holy orders introduces the Christian to a deeper sharing in Christ's ministry of the Word in the service of others. Matrimony assumes the spouses into that mystery of redemptive love by which Christ acquired the Church as his beloved bride (cf. Eph. 5:21-33).

Each sacrament pledges Christ's availability to enter upon a personal encounter. We need not look merely to the example given by the historical Christ; we can meet the living Christ himself under sacramental sign. All Christian life should, therefore, be sacramental in origin. To live in Christ, to be a son in the Son, to order our moral life according to the law which is Christ—all these mean a morality based on the sacraments. Each Christian needs to realize a sacramental life-project: through his actions to render vital the dynamic grace offered by Christ personally in each sacrament; to accept his consecration as a commission for a life of grace conformed to Christ; and never to make himself a living lie by perverting his sacramental configuration through sin. If the Christian accomplishes this, he fulfills the law of Christ. (See for the preceding C. O'Neill, *Meeting Christ in the Sacraments* [N.Y.: Alba House, 1964] and E. Schillebeeckx, *Christ the Sacrament of the Encounter with God* [N.Y.: Sheed & Ward, 1963].)

The life of grace communicated through the Church and the sacraments allows believers to share in Christ's own divine-human love for the Father and for all men. The law of the Spirit in Christ Jesus is the law of love (agape): "The whole law is summed up in love" (Rom. 13:9-10). A committed Christian who does not love is a contradiction in terms. Jesus views fraternal love as the distinguishing mark of his followers (John 13:34-35) and Christians are exhorted to love as Christ loved us and gave himself for us (Eph. 5:2). If Christians live according to the Law of Christ, taking Christ as the standard of moral conduct, they must therefore accept a life of service in behalf of their fellow men. Sonship in the Son cannot remain individualistic; it must of necessity reach out to all men. The Christian's moral task becomes that of living Christ-like love. In loving the neighbor, he is assured of loving Christ himself present in the needy: "I was hungry and you gave me to drink; I was a stranger and you made me welcome; naked and you clothed me, sick and you visited me, in prison and you came to see me. . . . I tell you solemnly, insofar as you did this to one of the least of these brothers of mine, you did it to me" (Matt. 25:35-36, 40).

Christian morality emerges as simultaneously a life of sonship in Christ, a morality of Christ-likeness, a sacramental morality, a morality of love. Each statement implies the others and is a different aspect of the whole. Love may be singled out as the primary Christ-like attitude, the dynamic principle which imparts to the whole Christian life its firmness, inner strength, and steadfast ordering of daily activities for other people toward full communion with the Father.

MORAL CONDUCT BASED ON CHRIST

The acceptance in faith of Jesus Christ as the focal point introduces a new perspective, posture and direction in the Christian moral life. The value system, framework of ethical reflection, and sensitivity of the believer in regard to the world and men should change once loyalty is given to Christ. Cultural and social conditioning will continue to exercise great influence. But a new, normative factor, Christ himself, also will bear influence. Jesus testifies to God's love for men and the world: the world is good; men are good, loved and redeemed. Confidence, hope and optimism should, therefore, characterize the general moral posture of the Christian. Pessimism about man, his sexuality, human institutions, or the world does not accord with the revelation of God's view of man and the world in Christ. Goodness itself has entered the world and taken hold of all men, who must adhere to this new power. The radical possibility of salvation, reconciliation, fraternal love has already been achieved. Freedom, not fate, governs man; man shapes his own future. Boldness, a sense of risk, a venturing toward progress: these attitudes should mark the believer. In these ways, Christ serves as a source of illumination for the moral life. (See J. Gustafson, *Christ and the Moral Life* [N.Y.: Harper & Row, 1968] 238-71; J. Fuchs, "Human, Humanist and Christian Morality," in *Human Values and Christian Morality,* 112-47.)

A further question arises: Can one arrive at specific moral directives by basing moral life on the person of Christ? Granted that creation and redemption in Christ make him our objective standard, how does a Christian reach personal assurance that concrete moral actions accord with this norm? How does a morality based on Christ's central role apply this, for example, to Vietnam, birth control, racial injustice, or poverty? Several complementary points may provide initial responses to these questions. The remainder of moral theology will serve to give a fuller answer.

The primary law of the Christian believer is the grace of the Holy Spirit. The Spirit enlightens and moves each person to understand and accept Christ. The believer should listen to the call of the Spirit, which urges him toward the performance of good actions. In this sense, the gifts of grace and love are in themselves the prime ways in which God draws us toward responding to his call at each moment. Now is always the moment of grace. The love of the Spirit instills in the responsive believer an openness and sensitivity to authentic love in action. The grace of the Spirit provides an inner power of discerning the manner of realizing love in the individual decision, thus giving an internal, unwritten norm. The written or external law remains indispensable, because we imperfectly possess the Spirit. Sacred Scripture indicates clearly, however, that these external norms are secondary and peripheral compared to the inner law of the Spirit. (See K. Rahner, *The Dynamic Element in the Church,* and N. Crotty, "Biblical Perspectives in Moral Theology," *Theological Studies* 26 [1965] 574-95, esp. 579-84.)

Besides this individual guidance, the Spirit of Jesus teaches through Sacred Scripture and tradition, in which totality is found, "that Gospel which is the source of all saving truth and moral teaching" (*Dogmatic Constitution on Divine Revelation,* n. 7). In the Scriptures, "the Father who is in heaven meets his children with great love and speaks with them; and the force and power in the Word of God is so great that it remains the support and energy of the Church, the strength of faith for her sons, the food of the soul, the pure and perennial source of spiritual life" (n. 21). Through this Word, the Christian finds concrete ways to make his life accord with the moral norm, Christ himself. The Holy Spirit continually assists the living teaching office of the Church in proposing this moral doctrine of the Gospel and works a free acceptance of this teaching in the believer. Sacred Scripture, tradition, and the Church thus combine to provide the believer with concrete guidance for the new life in Christ.

Sacred Scripture recognizes the perduring reality of the original creative order in the category of "re-establishment" or "restoration." For example, as a foundation for his exhortations to the Colossians and to the Ephesians, St. Paul refers to "the man renewed in Christ." He indicates that the renewal takes place "according to the image of his Creator" (Col. 3:10). In Paul's view, because Christians have risen with Christ as new creatures, the man originally intended by God in creation has been re-established. The man who bears the image of Christ is restored to that level intended in the divine creative purpose. Theologians uphold the continuing validity of recourse to this created order: the order of redemption in Christ has not destroyed the order of creation, but rather has restored it. The meaning of man has been brought to fullness in Christ; but man remains man, with his reasoning powers, his affective states, his relations to the world and to other persons, his sexuality and his abilities to project his future. By reflecting on the implications of man in his endowment and vital relationships, all of which have been assumed into the new law of the Spirit, the Christian can attain insight into his proper moral conduct. This process of human reflection on the meaning of man will always be aided by God's grace, for the order of grace alone exists. In coming to know specific moral obligations discerned by human reasoning on the created order, the Christian learns concrete applications of his new life in Christ. Common human experience thus retains a major place in Christian living. All that is authentically human comes under the law of Christ.

Can a morality based on our sonship in Christ provide specific norms for moral conduct? Yes, in the sense explained. The committed Christian will bring to his individual and social concerns a unique perspective, attitude, and life-orientation. The Holy Spirit will urge a Christ-like response at every moment. Scriptural insights interpreted in the living Christian community will cause him to stress the dignity of all men, the goodness of the world and human values, the primacy of love, freedom from sin and death, and openness to what God is working in the world. Reflective reasoning aided by grace will spell out the specific details of man's self-realization in, through, and with Christ.

BIBLIOGRAPHY

Bourdeau, F.-Danet, A., *Introduction to the Law of Christ* (N.Y.: Alba House, 1966).

Bouwman, G., *The Bible on the Imitation of Christ* (DePere, Wisconsin: St. Norbert Press, 1965).

Congar, Y., *Jesus Christ* (N.Y.: Herder & Herder, n.d.).

Fuchs, J., *Natural Law. A Theological Investigation* (N.Y.: Sheed & Ward, 1965).

————, *Human Values and Christian Morality* (Dublin: Gill and Macmillan, 1970).

Gilleman, G., *The Primacy of Charity in Moral Theology* (Paramus, N.J.: Newman, 1959), esp. 196-238.

Gillon, L., *Christ and Moral Theology* (N.Y.: Alba House, 1967).

Gustafson, J., *Christ and the Moral Life* (N.Y.: Harper & Row, 1968).

Häring, B., *The Law of Christ*, 3 vols. (Paramus, N.J.: Newman, 1961, 1963, 1966).

McDonagh, E.: see bibliography for Chapter III.

McNamara, K., "Life in Christ: Life in the Church," in *Moral Theology Renewed*, ed. E. McDonagh (Dublin: Gill & Son, 1965) 85-102.

O'Neill, C., *Meeting Christ in the Sacraments* (N.Y.: Alba House, 1964).

Schelkle, K. *Discipleship and Priesthood* (N.Y.: Herder & Herder, 1965).

Schillebeeckx, E., *Christ the Sacrament of the Encounter with God* (N.Y.: Sheed & Ward, 1963).

Schnackenburg, R., *Christian Existence in the New Testament*, 2 vols. (Notre Dame Univ., 1968-1969).

————, *The Moral Teaching of the New Testament* (N.Y.: Herder & Herder, 1965) 15-25, 43-53, 161-67, 307-22.

Spicq, C., *The Trinity and Our Moral Life According to St. Paul* (Paramus, N.J.: Newman, 1963).

Thils, G., *Christian Holiness* (Tielt: Lanoo Publishers, 1963) esp. 83-98.

Tillmann, F., *The Master Calls* (Baltimore: Helicon, 1961).

5. God Calls— Man Responds

Religion and morality draw their dominant themes and overall structure from the concept of God which inspires them. The history of religions shows the broad variance of these concepts, which range from an image of God as thunder, lightning, earthquake, or other impersonal forces of nature, to an image of the divine as the inexorable and wrathful Judge or Supreme Lawmaker. Taboo morality based on man-made graven images of the divine has consequently asserted itself recurrently in mankind's journey in history.

Christian moral theology should draw its themes and structure from divine revelation, which is God's self-manifestation and self-communication: his Word. The whole history of the record of revelation in Sacred Scripture follows a set structure: God initiates a loving relationship whereby he offers himself to man, and he invites man's response in return. It is basically a morality based on a covenant between God and man, a morality of community. It takes the form, therefore, of a personal and dialogical structure: God calls and man responds. God's Word is not a humanist construction of ethics, a clever technique for personal achievement and social balance. Biblical morality is instead a part of the drama of God's Word being accepted or rejected. God summons man; the human response is one of obedience or refusal. (See F. Bourdeau-A. Danet, *Introduction to the Law of Christ,* 93-94.)

GOD FOUNDS A COVENANT

The Old Testament records God's self-communication to man leading to his choice of a people. Yahweh initiates the covenantal

69

relationship and his love for his people retains a primacy in comparison to man's response. Yahweh's fidelity to his promises contrasts time and again with human infidelity and rebelliousness. From the time of the Exodus experience, the Jews were able to see this pattern in all God's dealings with man and they interpreted past events in this manner. For didactic purposes, they depicted God as manifesting himself to man from the very beginnings of creation in the persons of Adam and Eve, and as inviting faithfulness to himself. Man broke this dialogue, according to the Genesis account of the Fall, but the Lord patiently determined to renew it by the continual gift of himself. He aroused in man the hope of being saved (Gen. 3:15) and he ceaselessly kept the human race in his care.

Sacred Scripture recounts that, at the appointed time, the Lord extended to Abraham his promise of a covenant in perpetuity, "to be his God and the God of his descendants after him" (Gen. 17:19). Abraham put his faith in Yahweh, who counted this response as making him justified (Gen. 15:6) and considered him a friend (Isaiah 41:9). So commences an immense narration of God's saving interventions in behalf of his chosen people, mingled with man's response and infidelity. The Lord reveals his name to Moses and speaks with him "face to face, as a man speaks with his friend" (Ex. 33:11). Inviting Israel to close union, he delivers his people from Egypt and fulfills his promises by leading them into the promised land: "When Israel was a child I loved him, and I called my son out of Egypt" (Hosea 11:1). The relationship between Yahweh and his people emerges as so personal that the sacred authors introduce various images connoting this idea: Yahweh loves Israel as a husband loves his wife; or as a father his son; or as a person tends some treasured possession. (See W. Bouwmeester, *The Bible on the Covenant* [DePere, Wis.: St. Norbert Abbey, 1966] 33-51.)

The Lord's choice of his people is characterized by gratuitous mercy and love. In gratuitously choosing Israel, however, he expects them to recognize him as the only holy and powerful God, which presumes that they submit to his moral demands. Even in communicating the Ten Commandments (Ten Words or Decalogue), however, Yahweh speaks words of love, citing his past saving deeds of love: "I am Yahweh your God who brought you

out of the land of Egypt. . . . You shall have no gods except me"
(Ex. 20:1-2). "If Yahweh set his heart on you and chose you,
it was not because you outnumbered other peoples: you were the
least of all peoples. It was for love of you and to keep the oath
he swore to your fathers that Yahweh brought you out with his
right hand and redeemed you from the house of slavery. . . . You
are therefore to keep and observe the commandments and stat-
utes and ordinances that I lay down for you today" (Deut. 7:7-8,
11).

These loving interventions of Yahweh are intended to elicit a
total response of love and obedience to his will: "And now, Israel,
what does Yahweh your God ask of you? Only this: to fear
Yahweh your God, to follow all his ways, to love him, to serve
Yahweh your God with all your heart and all your soul, to keep
the commandments and laws of Yahweh that for your good I
lay down for you today" (Deut. 10:12-13). The whole life of
Israel is destined by the Lord to develop as a response of love to
his words of love. Israel's inconstancy, however, recurs time and
again. "Israel is repeatedly unfaithful, yet this adulterous bride
keeps returning time after time to her husband. This must be in
accord with the plan of the Lord. He punishes her, he periodically
abandons her to her own responses—but he never leaves her
completely (Hos. 3:1-4), for he is a faithful God. Perennially,
his Word perdures and his plan to make Israel a holy people
prevails" (Bouwmeester, 75).

This Hebrew covenant morality possessed a unique and specific
character which stood in sharp contrast to Greek notions of morality. "Whereas for the Greeks the object of morality was personal fulfillment and social equilibrium, for the Hebrew it was
a dialogue with Yahweh founded on the historical revelation of
Yahweh's will, which Israel remained free to accept or reject.
For the Greek philosopher sin was an error estranging man from
the rule of objective law or custom and had little or no relationship to the divine will. For the Hebrew it had an essentially religious character. Morality for the Greek was found in order of
judgment. For the Hebrew it resided in the order of acts insofar
as these manifest a fundamental attitude before God. To qualify
this attitude as good or bad, biblical man did not refer to man's
nature or to the dictates of conscience, but to the objective will of

God manifested in the law. Fundamentally this attitude consisted in man's responses to the covenant" (E. LaVerdiere, "Covenant Morality," *Worship* 38 [1964] 240-46, at 243).

One serious distortion in post-exilic Israel was the tendency to view the moral life as centered on observance of the Law rather than as a response to God's will. Reliance on an impersonal law, the Torah, replaced the covenantal theme of a deep interpersonal relationship between Yahweh and his people. The civil, cultural, and moral precepts of the Law received equal stress, while the underlying values and the religious dimensions became secondary. Jesus reacted against the legalism implied in this outlook, upbraiding the Pharisees, who "tie up heavy burdens and lay them on men's shoulders" (Matt. 23:4). (See N. Crotty, "Biblical Perspectives in Moral Theology," *Theological Studies* 26 [1965] 574-95, at 577.)

THE WORD BECAME FLESH

God's communication of himself to man reached its climax in Christ, the Word made flesh: "At various times in the past and in various different ways, God spoke to our ancestors through the prophets; but in our own time, the last days, he has spoken to us through his Son" (Heb. 1:1-2). This divine intervention in human history was a true manifestation of God demanding man's attention, reception, and response.

The Word, the fullness of revelation, announces the total divine love for men in the mysteries of his redemptive actions: the incarnation, passion, death, resurrection, and ascension. Christ in his very person, with all his actions, words, sufferings, commandments, is the abiding Word of God delivered to man. This divine presence in Jesus changed man totally and irrevocably, demanding man's recognition, not only intellectually but in his whole life. The Word of Love invited human love in response. In this Word Incarnate, the God-man, human response is realized perfectly and the proper response of every individual man to God's personal call becomes visible. The definitive answer to God's call has been spoken in Jesus and men need but respond in the same fashion. Hence, the divine self-disclosure in the Son is a gift or call inviting man and is, at the same time, a demand enjoined on man for a response through a life of love worthy of this gift of love. The Word made flesh thus epitomizes in his person the call-response structure of God's dealings with man; he is in himself the New Covenant. If moral life centers on the person of Christ, therefore, it should follow a call-response structure. (See E. McDonagh, "Moral Theology Renewed," *Irish Ecclesiastical Record* 104 [1965] 321-32, at 322).

Jesus' preaching embodies this pattern of call-response. Faith, trust, full commitment to his person and doctrine, personal love of him should characterize the disciple. Nothing less than a total yes should be the reply. E. Thurneysen states: "The sayings of the Sermon on the Mount, like all sayings of Jesus, are to be understood as dialogue, i.e., as an obligating and liberating word of address from him who wishes to come to expression in them, in order that we should become those who answer to him with our whole life" (*The Sermon on the Mount,* 13; see also Y. Congar, *Jesus Christ,* chap. IV, "The Preaching of Christ," which shows the dialogical structure of the parables of Jesus).

St. Paul's Teaching

St. Paul repeatedly utilizes the theme of God's call and man's response in connection with the new life in Christ. "We may say that the whole Christian existence can be summarized in the fact that they have been called: for Paul 'the called' very often simply means the faithful" (J. DeFraine, *The Bible on Vocation and Election* [DePere: St. Norbert Abbey, 1966] 36-37.) This calling of God is a technical term for the completely divine character of God's initiative, for he creates out of nothing and "calls into existence the things that do not exist" (Rom. 4:17). Following this notion, St. Paul refers to his own apostleship as a personal vocation (Rom. 1:1; 1 Cor. 1:1) and he presupposes that all priesthood is a special calling from God. God himself is described as freely calling whomever he wants (Rom. 4:17) and as choosing the predestined (Rom. 8:28-30). He takes for granted that all Christians have an awareness of their call in Christ (Rom. 1:6-7; 1 Cor. 1:9; Eph. 1:11), leading to the grace of Christ (Gal. 1:6, 15) and Christian freedom (Gal. 5:13).

The dynamic nature and gratuity of God's call receive repeated emphasis in Paul's theology. "The Holy God continually calls his elect. Vocation and election are not to be considered an acquired possession; they always remain an unmerited and unmeritable grace, a continually renewed initiative of the divine Father who wants to save. Even though Paul seems to present vocation as a state of having been called, this must be considered an effect of God's active calling" (DeFraine, 3).

Pauline theology passes from the enunciation of various indicatives (e.g., you *are* called, holy, free) to exhortation of the consequent moral imperatives (e.g., you are called by God, so you *ought to live* according to his will). "I . . . implore you therefore to lead a life worthy of your vocation" (Eph. 4:1), exhorts the apostle. "What God wants is for you all to be holy. . . . We have been called by God to be holy, not to be immoral" (1 Thess. 4:3, 7). Paul does not have a monolithic concept of God's call, however, for he states that "everybody has his own particular gifts from God, one with a gift for the opposite" (1 Cor. 7:7). Every Christian's life, whatever his particular occupation, thus emerges as an exalted personal calling from God himself, a gift which invites a personal response in the practical details of life. (See J. Fuchs, *Human Values and Christian Morality*, 10.)

CALLED TO WORSHIP

The incarnation was the consecration of Christ through the anointing in the Holy Spirit. His sacrificial death was the supreme act of priesthood in conformity to his Father's will and the preparation for the priestly consecration of the Church as a whole and of every individual Christian. As the visible extension of the living and glorious Christ, the Church is the living Word, drawing her life from his redemptive words and deeds. She communicates the Word to men, serving as a sign of God's continuing call to salvation. Herself called as the body of the Lord, the Church responds to God in Christ as the worshiping community of salvation. The call-response pattern of salvation history is thus verified in the Church herself. Christians, as true hearers of the Word, should listen for God's Word addressed through the

Church. Through this "holy gathering of those called" (Rom. 1:7; 1 Cor. 1:2), the faithful can themselves call upon the Lord and respond to his Word.

Specifically through the sacramental action of the Church, God calls men to himself by assimilating them to Christ the High Priest, making them capable of worshiping him in every dimension of their existence and impelling them to conform their wills to the will of the Father, as Christ did. All Christians, whether ordained or non-ordained, become true priests through baptism: "You are a chosen race, a royal priesthood, a people set apart to sing the praises of God who called you out of the darkness into his wonderful light. Once you were not a people at all and now you are the people of God" (1 Pet. 2:9-10). This sacramental consecration constitutes a true call to priestly worship as the proper response of the Christian's life. As sacramental men, the baptized should live out their call to worship by viewing all activities as acts of worship in and through Christ: "Set yourselves close to him so that you too, the holy priesthood that offers the spiritual sacrifices which Jesus Christ has made acceptable to God, may be living stones making a spiritual house" (1 Pet. 2:5). The Christian people should thus be the new Temple consecrated to the Lord.

This dialogical movement of call-response takes place in the fullest sense through the sacred liturgy, especially the Eucharist, where God calls us under sacred signs to respond to his Word. "The structural pattern of the liturgy closely resembles that of salvation history, in that throughout we see a dialectic of revelation and response, the great God revealing himself as agape (1 John 4:8), seeking to evoke a response of faith from man. In Scripture we read of the *magnalia Dei,* the wonderful saving events of God, placing himself at the service of man for man's salvation. Through the liturgy this saving action continues to be present in history. And just as man was called to commitment by God through these saving events in the past, so too he is still being called to commitment by God through these same saving acts sacramentally present today. God's revelation of saving service calls man to a response of saving service on his part" (D. Gray, "Liturgy and Morality," *Worship* 39 [1965] 28-35, at 29).

The liturgy should, then, play a central role in Christian moral life: "The liturgy is . . . the outstanding means by which the faithful can express in their lives, and manifest to others, the mystery of Christ and the real nature of the true Church" (*Constitution on the Sacred Liturgy*, n. 2). "The liturgy is the summit toward which the activity of the Church is directed; at the same time it is the fountain from which all her power flows" (n. 10). In short, the liturgy is "the fountain" whereby we hear God's call (his Word in various words and events), and "the summit" of the Church's continuous response through Christ for the sake of his called people. This response is realized most fully in our Eucharistic union with Christ, where we strive in a special way for that conformity to the Father's will which marked Jesus' life and which should characterize Christian living.

PERSONAL MORALITY

Christian morality is more than saving one's soul, being virtuous, striving for happiness, or keeping the commandments. These approaches may, in fact, imply a certain self-centeredness, for they may foster an excessive concern with the self, leading to an egotistical morality foreign to Christ's teaching. Rather than viewing morality as a dialogue between God and man, these systems may remain on the level of monologue: man to himself and within himself. Though these notions retain some value for Christian life, none of them is the main structural theme of moral theology based on revelation. A call-response structure for morality, on the other hand, seems apt to describe the personal relation of persons, I-Thou, which exists between the living God and the man called in Christ. This embodies St. John's insight: "God is love, and he who abides in love abides in God, and God in him" (1 John 4:16). Recalling the personal relationship between God and man which Christ revealed in his person, deeds, and words, St. Paul writes: "The spirit you received is not the spirit of slaves bringing fear into your lives again; it is the spirit of sons, and it makes us cry out, 'Abba, Father!' " (Rom. 8:15). In many ways, the original and startling substance of Jesus' message was his presentation of God as a Father immediately pres-

ent, as near as a human father to his child, and so understanding
that our every need concerns him before our expressing it: "If
you, then, who are evil, know how to give your children what is
good, how much more will your Father in heaven give good things
to those who ask him" (Matt. 7:11).

Reflection on this call-response structure shows that no Christian should order his moral life according to merely impersonal
objective norms or commands. All norms and commands receive their value because they enunciate the call of the three Divine Persons to human persons. God's commandments mediate
the personal love addressed by God and the proper response of
man should be love: "Love . . . is the fulfillment of the law"
(Rom. 12:10). A personalist morality of call-response views
compliance with a law or command as the obedient response to
God himself, instead of submission to some impersonal force.
Man's response will, moreover, be responsible knowledge and
love, not a blind obedience which diminishes the role of human
reason. The very core of moral decision is saying yes to God's
calls, however they are expressed. This requires humble and
docile attentiveness to God. Often it is completed by faltering
or by bold hazard of choice among myriad possibilities that lie
open before one. The responsive Christian cannot evade personal responsibility before God through recourse to human
authority alone. Neither an Eichmann-like assent to genocide nor
an eyes-closed submission to religious authority suffices. The believer is accountable for his obedience, for he has a God-given
intellect and a free will. Even the seeking of counsel from a priest
or actual obedience to Church law can never serve as an absolute excuse for shirking personal responsibility. Seeking counsel
and obedience assist in exhausting possibilities in preparation
for the decision of conscience for which the individual person is
altogether responsible.

How can a believer make this call-response structure a conscious theme for his own life? Through prayerful reflection on
God's ways of approaching man, he will realize that God is not
simply Someone or Something which awaits him as the goal and
judge of his life-work. God is three Persons who say something
every day and who deserve an answer in action. The true believer is a person who meets God, someone in whose life God has

entered. Like the Jews of the Old Testament, the Christian will grow to detect the message of the Lord in all creation; the child of God will see in events and in people the Word of the Father. Aware that God the Father has created the earth and all worldly values in Christ, the believer will take his tasks seriously and will endeavor to realize through his cooperation God's personal plan for him. He will view his love for his wife and children, his manual labor, teaching or clerical work, his golfing, hunting or watching television as possibilities of growth in continuous response to God's calls, wherever he discovers them. Living in close contact with the Spirit, he will find that "all things work together for good," for whether he eats, or drinks, or sleeps, he does all for the glory of God.

The Christian believer becomes like a lover who has met the girl he loves—his life is turned upside down. Until this point, he was alone even when among others; henceforth he becomes even more aware of his true self and he now views his own life in terms of the other person. So with the Christian, whose life is no longer an insipid or meaningless destiny, nor an impersonal fate. It is a route outlined by Someone who calls to him by walking before him.

I exist from now on with him. He expects from me a certain kind of life. Nothing in my life is unimportant to him, and I must live for his glory by responding to his desires. Our life unfolds in the night of faith. God attacks, we repel, we struggle, we fight. But from the start of this encounter, we are marked as men of God and for God. We live our life together in dialogue, in continuous conversation—in the realization of his call and our response. (Adapted from F. Bourdeau-A. Danet, *Introduction to the Law of Christ,* 94-95.)

BIBLIOGRAPHY

Bourdeau, F.-Danet, A., *Introduction to the Law of Christ* (N.Y.: Alba House, 1966).

Bouwmeester, W., *The Bible on the Covenant* (DePere, Wis.: St. Norbert Abbey, 1966).

Crotty, N., "Biblical Perspectives in Moral Theology," *Theological Studies* 26 (1965) 574-96.

DeFraine, J., *The Bible on Vocation and Election* (DePere, Wis.: St. Norbert Abbey, 1966).

Gray, D., "Liturgy and Morality," *Worship* 39 (1965) 28-35.

Häring, B., *The Law of Christ,* Vol. I (Paramus, N.J.: Newman, 1961) 35-97, 252-66; Vol. II (1963) xxi-xxxviii, 126-29.

LaVerdiere, E., "Covenant Morality," *Worship* 38 (1964) 240-46.

O'Neill, C., "What Is Liturgical Spirituality?" *Cross and Crown* 17 (1965) 34-45.

Schelkle, K., *Discipleship and Priesthood* (N.Y.: Herder & Herder, 1965) 9-32.

Stevens, P., "Moral Theology and the Liturgy," *Yearbook of Liturgical Studies* 1 (1960) 65-122.

6. Free To Love

Freedom and love should characterize the new people of God. Vatican II presents these values as distinguishing marks: "The heritage of this people are the dignity and freedom of the sons of God, in whose hearts the Holy Spirit dwells as in his temple. Its law is the new commandment to love as Christ loved us" (*Dogmatic Constitution on the Church*, n. 9). These words of the Council re-echo central teachings of the New Testament, found especially in the writings of St. John and St. Paul. Jesus of Nazareth lived and proclaimed a new freedom from sin, coercive law, and meaningless death. His disciples should manifest their freedom by a life of loving service to the neighbor. Christians are free to love. The biblical and theological understanding of this statement provides further insight into the new life in Christ.

CHRISTIAN FREEDOM

Böckle, F., *Law and Conscience* (N.Y.: Sheed & Ward, 1966) 23-48.

Crotty, N., "Biblical Perspectives in Moral Theology," *Theological Studies* 26 (1965) 574-96, esp. 579-84.

Fitzmyer, J., "Saint Paul and the Law," *The Jurist* 27 (1967) 18-36.

Häring, B., *The Law of Christ* Vol. 1 (Paramus, N.J.: Newman, 1961) 257-63.

Lyonnet, S., "Liberté du chrétien," in *Morale humaine. Morale chrétienne* (Paris: Desclee de Brouwer, 1966) 213-21.

————, *St. Paul: Liberty and Law* (Rome: Pontifical Biblical Institute, 1962).

————, "Saint Paul: Liberty and Law," in *Readings in Biblical Morality,* ed. C. Salm (N.Y.: Prentice-Hall, 1967) 62-83; condensed in *Theology Digest* 11 (1963) 12-18.

Schnackenburg, R., *Christian Existence in the New Testament*, Vol. II (Notre Dame Univ., 1969) 31-53.

————, *The Moral Teaching of the New Testament* (N.Y.: Herder & Herder, 1965), 275-77, 347-53.

Spicq, C., *Charity and Liberty* (N.Y.: Alba House, 1965).

"If you make my Word your home you will indeed be my disciples, you will learn the truth and the truth will make you free" (John 8:31-32). This saying of Jesus indicates the paradoxical element of Christian freedom: to possess the freedom of the sons of God one must accept in radical obedience the will of the Father manifested in Jesus, who is truth for all men. Jesus gives constant obedience to the will of the Father out of total love, and does nothing of himself (John 6:36; 8:28). This filial acceptance of the Father's will motivated by love constitutes the source of his freedom, for he thereby transcends all enslaving powers which alienate man. He incarnates full, personal freedom in complete openness to the Father: "The Father loves me, because I lay down my life in order to take it up again. No one takes it from me; I lay it down of my own free will, and as it is in my power to lay it down, so it is in my power to take it up again; and this is the command I have been given by my Father" (John 10:17-18).

Having become obedient even to death, Jesus won for all men the possibility of experiencing the freedom resulting from loving acceptance of the Father's will. The freedom of the sons of God does not, therefore, bring independence from God or permit arbitrariness in moral conduct. It does not foster a breakdown in moral responsibility. It leads the committed disciple to embrace in love the will of the Father as made known in Christ. The freedom which Jesus experienced thus becomes a Christian inheritance.

St. Paul sees a threefold freedom resulting from the new life in Christ: a freedom from sin, from the Law, and from death: "The reason, therefore, why those who are in Christ Jesus are not condemned is that the law of the spirit of life in Christ Jesus has set you free from the law of sin and death" (Rom. 8:1-2). This freedom from sin is not only a freedom from guilt and punishment from past transgressions, but freedom also from the bondage of concupiscience and from the slavery of one's own desires. Man experiences freedom from the state of estrangement from God and from the wrath of God. Slavery to righteousness, to the Father's will, replaces slavery to sin. (See Romans 6, the entire chapter.)

The Christian also obtains freedom from the Jewish Law and all external, compelling law. Paul's attitude toward the Law points out its anomaly. On the one hand, the Law is holy, righteous, and good (Rom. 7:12) and even spiritual (Rom. 7:14), since it ultimately came from God and was destined by him to lead men to the new life of communion with God. The apostle emphasizes the Israelites' obligation to observe the Law as a norm for life. On the other hand, the Jewish Law is depicted as incapable by its own power of producing the uprightness which was its destiny: "No one can be justified in the sight of God by keeping the Law" (Rom. 3:20). In fact, the Law has acted as an occasion of sin, for it brought out man's rebelliousness against God's positive will: "Once, when there was no Law, I was alive; but when the commandment came, sin came to life and I died: the commandment was meant to lead me to life but it turned out to mean death for me" (Rom. 7:9-11). Sin itself has become a law (Rom. 7:25), keeping man in bondage and slavery through the very Mosaic Law which God had intended as a means of educating his people that it might come of age to learn of Christ. This Law no longer has a claim on the Christian: as Christ by his death put an end to the Law, so the Christian has died to the Law. This freedom looses the Christian from all legalistic righteousness such as flourished in the Pharisaic tradition with its 613 commands and prohibitions. "The Christian who is led by the Spirit finds himself freed, in Christ, from the Law of Moses; he is free from it not only as the Law of Moses, but as law. He is delivered from any law that constrains or coerces (I do not say binds) him from without; yet, this in no way makes him an amoral being, outside the realm of good and evil" (S. Lyonnet, "Saint Paul: Liberty and Law," *Theology Digest* 11 [1963] 12).

Freedom from eternal death is the third freedom Paul ascribes to the new life in Christ. Sin can claim victory only in eternal death. Set free from sin, however, the Christian awaits eternal life in Christ: "You have been set free from sin, you have been made slaves of God, and you get a reward leading to your sanctification and ending in eternal life. For the wage paid by sin is death; the present given by God is eternal life in Christ Jesus our Lord" (Rom. 6:22-23). In the power of the Risen Lord, the Christian can face death with hope; death loses its sting. (See R. Schnackenburg, *Christian Existence in the New Testament*, Vol. II, 38-40, on this point.)

Delivered from the law of sin and death, the Christian is open to the law of the life-giving Spirit. Through the infusion of the Holy Spirit, in contrast to the letter of the law and Jewish tradition, the life of the Christian is governed. This new, inner source of spiritual energy constitutes the only law which imposes a real obligation on the faithful Christian. Paul uses the term "law" in a figurative sense, it is true, but it aptly describes the new unwritten norm of conduct which motivates, energizes, and vitalizes the Christian. This Pauline meaning for the law of the Spirit is otherwise known as grace itself, by which Christ introduces us to the Father and gives us the Spirit. The principle of Christian activity is no longer merely an external list of do's and don'ts, but rather the internal guidance of the dynamic Spirit which enables the Christian to cry "Abba, Father" and which testifies to him that he is a child of God (Gal. 4:6; Rom. 8:15). "The new Christian liberty that Paul is referring to will be clear to us if we remember its orientation (freedom *to* . . .) and its possibility (by the Holy Ghost . . .). We already possess the freedom to do good (that is, moral freedom) through the Holy Spirit, who impels us from within, guiding us and giving us the victory over the sarx (flesh)" (R. Schnackenburg, *The Moral Teaching of the New Testament*, 276; cf. 201-02). The Christian is no longer earthbound flesh when activated by this new law, but is now himself spiritual. Sin, evil, disorder, or transgression should not enter the Christian's life: "We are dead to sin, so how can we continue to live in it?" (Rom. 6:2).

This law of the Spirit of life brings freedom under the law of love. The Holy Spirit impels the Christian to use his freedom only to opt for God and for his neighbor. "The highest degree of freedom is the perfect love of God in which man makes himself free from whatsoever resistance to being led by the Holy Spirit and thus comes to self-mastery in obedience, in his service to God. He who lets himself be led completely by the Spirit of God, he is the truly free man, for 'the Lord is the Spirit, and where the Spirit of the Lord is, there is freedom' (2 Cor. 3:17)" (F. Böckle, *Fundamental Concepts of Moral Theology*, 27). Love itself becomes "the fulfillment of the Law" (Gal. 5:14; Rom. 13:8-10) and governs the Christian as his prime value. What does not express love does not lead to life in Christ: "If you love your fellow men you have carried out your obligations. All the commandments: you shall not commit adultery, you shall not kill, you shall not steal, you shall not covet, and so on, are summed up in this single command: You must love your neighbor as yourself. Love is the one thing that cannot hurt your neighbor; that is why it is the answer to every one of the commandments" (Rom. 13:8-10).

Christian freedom has no parallel, therefore, with some contemporary meanings assigned the term freedom, which have an egocentric connotation. Pleasure for pleasure's sake as a moral principle, or a general permissiveness in sexuality and personal conduct, finds no basis in the freedom of the sons of God proclaimed in the New Testament. The Spirit directs Christian freedom to active participation in the community, so that the body of Christ might be built up through loving service. The growth of other persons, not an ethics of selfishness, is the aim of Christ's liberating activity.

S. Lyonnet expresses the underlying reason which leads St. Paul to this equiparation between the law of the Spirit and the law of love: "In a morality defined essentially in relation to a norm proposed from without, the good is what conforms to this norm, evil is what does not conform. On the other hand, in a morality defined in relation to an interior demand, the very activity of the Holy Spirit in us, there will necessarily be a demand of love, because the Holy Spirit is none other than the reciprocal love of the Father and the Son, the love by which the Father loves the Son and all humanity, which he has assumed, the love

which the Son in his priestly prayer asked his Father to communicate to us: 'That the love with which you have loved me
may be in them and I in them'" (S. Lyonnet, "Liberté du
chrétien," in *Morale humaine. Morale chrétienne,* 216).

Having reduced the new law to love, St. Paul can say: "If
you are guided by the Spirit you will be in no danger of yielding
to self-indulgence, since self-indulgence is the opposite of the
Spirit. If you are led by the Spirit, no law can touch you" (Gal.
5:16-18). Nothing could be more obvious to St. Paul, because
the Spirit and the flesh are two antagonistic principles: if the
Christian follows the one, he opposes the other. A fully spiritual
person, a Christian completely led by the Holy Spirit, will avoid
evil by instinct without needing an external, written law. He fulfills every law in the full freedom of the sons of God, even
though he is freed from every compelling rule of conduct imposed from without. When he opens himself fully to the guidance
of the Holy Spirit, then, the Christian is not "under the Law"
(Rom. 6:14) and yet he leads a perfect moral life.

Is there no place for law in Christian morals? Does New Testament theology invalidate the recourse to any law in favor of the
law of love alone? The author of 1 Timothy succinctly states
the governing principle of his insight: "Laws are not framed for
people who are good. On the contrary, they are for criminals
and revolutionaries, for the irreligious and the wicked, for the
sacrilegious and the irreverent" (1 Tim. 1:8-9). In his teaching,
"if all Christians were just, there would be no need to restrain
them by law. Law, as a rule, does not enter upon the scene except to arrest disorder" (S. Lyonnet, "Saint Paul . . ." *Theology
Digest* 11 [1963] 17). The fervent Christian most often will fulfill the law, without adverting to the fact. On the other hand,
as soon as the inner tendency toward moral goodness no longer
exerts influence, the law is there to guide him and to warn him
that he is no longer led by the Spirit. In this latter case, the
law will play the role of a teacher, leading the Christian to Christ.
It will help him to recognize his condition as a sinner who has
escaped the power of the Spirit. The external law will ensure
true discernment of "the fruit of the Spirit" from "the works of
the flesh" (Gal. 5:16-26).

According to St. Paul, then, the law of love would be the sole guide for the totally just person, the Christian fully responsive to the guidance of the Holy Spirit. A realistic appraisal of Christians, however, brought home to the apostle the difference between the ideal and real condition of believers. "Although he is in the state of grace, that is, led by the Holy Spirit, the Christian, as long as he remains on earth, possesses the Spirit only imperfectly, as a sort of pledge (Rom. 8:23; 2 Cor. 1:22). . . . He is never so completely free from sin and from the flesh that he cannot any moment fall back under their sway. Now in this unstable position, the law—the external, written, objective norm of man's conduct—will guide him in distinguishing the works of the flesh from the fruit of the Spirit. . . . Until the Christian acquires full spiritualization in heaven, there will remain alongside grace . . . a secondary element, no more able to justify than was the Old Law, but still indispensable for sinners and by no means superfluous for the just who are still imperfect" (S. Lyonnet, "Saint Paul . . ." *Theology Digest* 11 [1963] 17).

The law of the Spirit of life in Christ Jesus far surpasses the minimal demands of any external norms of behavior. Grace moves the Christian beyond the letter of the law and a code morality to accomplish the ideals set forth by Jesus. Love makes its claims on the attentive Christian and law does not occupy a central position. This does not, however, imply that the minimal requirement of moral norms do not bind the Christian. External law retains its binding force and is still indispensable in our pilgrim state. Christian formulations of moral norms in Scripture and in the Christian community, particularly by the teaching office of the Church, mark out the boundaries of the area within which the Christian should express his love. This marginal and secondary character of external law does not render it irrelevant for Christian behavior. Love, not law, should be the focal point of moral effort, but external commandments can truly safeguard the exercise of Christian liberty. However, "since the sole aim of the external law is to safeguard the Christian's inner dynamism, it derives all its value from the latter, not the other way around" (S. Lyonnet, "Saint Paul . . ." *Theology Digest* 11 [1963] 18). Obedience to law becomes the exteriority of love.

St. Paul's specific exhortations and recommendations to the early Christian communities take on a different sense in light of this understanding. He expresses not so much a code or a norm to be exploited and interpreted casuistically, as rather various examples of the Christian principle of love reacting to communal situations. Norms for individual conduct are subsumed under one notion: under love, under concern for others, under the dynamic demand of Christian communal living. Love fulfills the whole Mosaic Law and any other external norm of conduct because it impels man to seek the good of others, which is the prime aim of any moral norm. The works of the flesh will cease: "fornication, gross indecency and sexual irresponsibility; idolatry and sorcery; feuds and wrangling, jealousy, bad temper and quarrels; disagreements, factions, envy; drunkenness, orgies and similar things." The Spirit will bring far different conduct: "love, joy, peace, patience, kindness, goodness, trustfulness, gentleness and self-control" (Gal. 5:19-23). (See J. Fitzmyer, "Saint Paul and the Law," *The Jurist* 27 [1967] 29-36.)

CHRISTIAN CHARITY

Barrosse, T., *Christianity: Mystery of Love* (Notre Dame, Ind.: Fides, 1964).

Carpentier, R., "Le primat de l'amour dans la vie morale," *Nouvelle Révue Théologique* 83 (1961) 3-24, 255-70.

Gilleman, G., *The Primacy of Charity in Moral Theology* (Paramus, N.J.: Newman, 1959).

McDonagh, E., "The Primacy of Charity," in *Moral Theology Renewed,* ed. E. McDonagh (Dublin: Gill and Son, 1965), 130-50.

Rahner, K., "Reflections on the Unity of the Love of Neighbour and the Love of God," in *Theological Investigations,* Vol. 6 (Baltimore: Helicon, 1969) 231-49; summarized in *Theology Digest* 15 (1967) 87-93.

Schnackenburg, R., *The Moral Teaching of the New Testament* (N.Y.: Herder & Herder, 1965), 90-109, 217-25, 316-29.

Spicq, C., *Agape in the New Testament*, 3 vols. (St. Louis: B. Herder, 1963, 1965, 1966).

The freedom to love which Paul preaches finds its roots in Jesus' own person, words and deeds. Christianity has been rightly convinced that the greatest of Jesus' achievements in the moral sphere was his teaching on love. This message, whose highest expression is the mission of God's Son to redeem sinful man, brought something new into the world, an idea and a reality so vast and incomprehensible as to be God's prime revelation. Compared to non-Christian ethics, whether Epicurean, utilitarian, or sentimental, Christian morality possesses a unique element: all morality may be summed up in a generous and universal love of God and every man, centered on the person of Christ. (Cf. R. Schnackenburg, *The Moral Teaching of the New Testament*, 90-91.)

God's Gift

Christians should not forget that the charity which occupies a primacy in the Christian life stems from God, not from man's own natural powers. God's love for man awakens in him the capacity to love him and his fellow men in return: "Let us love one another since love comes from God and everyone who loves is begotten by God and knows God" (1 John 4:7). The Holy Spirit bestows this power to love as God loves: "The love of God has been poured into our hearts by the Holy Spirit which has been given us" (Rom. 5:5). Man becomes like to God himself in sharing this divine love. But this love always remains God's gift. Charity reduces ultimately to God himself. As E. McDonagh states: "Charity is God's love abroad in the world. It is the presence of God in love to the human person, asking for love in response. It is the presence of God in love within the human person, seeking expression through his human and personal activity. It was in Christ that this loving presence of God to man and man's loving response achieved supreme realization. It is by each man's union with Christ that the divine love enters his heart and elicits his response" ("The Primacy of Charity," in *Moral Theology Renewed*, ed. E. McDonagh, 136).

A New Commandment

The great commandment of Jesus announces that the entire

new life in him finds its fulfillment in man's loving response to God's gift of love: "You must love the Lord your God with all your heart, with all your soul, and wtih all your mind. This is the greatest and the first commandment. The second resembles it: You must love your neighbor as yourself. On these two commandments hang the whole Law, and the Prophets also" (Matt. 22:37-40). This teaching of Jesus has a basic originality which may be analyzed under several aspects. (See R. Schnackenburg, *The Moral Teaching of the New Testament,* 90-109, for a scholarly exposition of this material.)

First, Jesus revealed the indissoluble interior bond existing between love of God and love of neighbor. Love of God should find expression and give practical proof of itself in the equally important brotherly love and, conversely, brotherly love has love of God as its foundation and support.

Second, Jesus showed that the whole law could be reduced to this and only this chief commandment. The new life he offers expresses itself in love for God and for the neighbor, in a boundless manner, and issues from the depths of the person.

Third, Jesus interpreted love of one's neighbor as "love for the nearest person," that is, he extended love to all men without distinction. This startling teaching cuts across all racial boundaries and social castes, presupposing a universality of love that does not derive from a noble humanism, as in Hellenism. Nor does it venture hesitantly and reluctantly outside a closed circle, as in Judaism. Instead, the love preached by Jesus and expected of his disciples is fired by God's own all-embracing and all-merciful love.

Apart from the great commandment, Jesus nowhere spoke explicitly about loving God, though he implies this often when he refers to the filial attitude men should have toward God. This remarkable fact becomes more understandable upon further reflection. The parallel command of Jesus about brotherly love indicates a broad field of practical application for love of God. Love of man assumes the significance of a test of one's real love of God. Genuine love of God implies love-in-action toward the neighbor. Jesus' words about the proper dispositions for worshiping God show the point clearly: "If you are bringing your offering to the altar and there remember that your brother has something against you, leave your offering there before the altar, go and be reconciled with your brother first, and then come back and present your offering" (Matt. 5:23-24). The love of God which Jesus proclaimed, then, is not a mere feeling, an emotion, nor mystical happiness which remains on the purely internal level of pious thoughts and attitudes. Love of God never exists without love of the men living here on earth. St. John sums up the doctrine in strong language: "Anyone who says, 'I love God,' and hates his brother, is a liar, since a man who does not love the brother that he can see cannot love God, whom he has never seen. So this is the commandment that he has given us, that anyone who loves God must also love his brother" (1 John 4:20-21). Yves Congar can say: "The love which I have conceived for him has, we might say, its locus in the world in the love which I have for my neighbor. In this kind of created extension of God in his living images, I can do him the good that is demanded by my love for him. In this sense, God has, so to speak, given me my neighbor to love in his place. . . . In the Gospel revelation, not only does the love of God seem linked to the love of neighbor, but it is somehow enveloped by it" (Y. Congar, *Jesus Christ*, 74).

Karl Rahner has reached the heights of theological reflection in holding that the radical identity of love of God and love of neighbor alluded to in the biblical data finds its ontological justification in transcendental metaphysics. Explicit and thematic love of God, that is, love of him as a person and conceived after the manner of other persons we encounter, becomes possible only by a trusting, loving openness toward the whole of reality that occurs in love of neighbor. The primary and original love of God is not an explicit and categorical love, but rather a noncategorical and transcendental unthematic love of him. In other terms, in a non-conceptual way the virtue of divine charity bears us directly toward God, allowing us to love him with his own love. The virtue does not, however, give us a conceptual picture of God as a person. In the Johannine sense, we do not "see" (conceive) God; we "see" (conceive) the neighbor. The non-conceptual love of God renders possible our explicit and categorical love of the neighbor in Christ, for only God's love can equip us with the capacity to love other persons supernaturally. The living human experience of this explicit and conceptual love of the neighbor as a person in and for Christ then founds the possibility for us to have an explicit and conceptual love for God as a person. This interdependence and ontological unity of both loves implies the fullest reciprocity in the relationship: all true love of man is also charity toward God; all true love of God is also charity toward the neighbor. In the most complete sense, the love of God and the love of man are one virtue. The transcendent God meets man in man, in the service of one's brothers. (See K. Rahner, "The Unity of Love of God and Love of Neighbor," *Theology Digest* 15 [1967] 87-93; *id., Theological Investigations,* Vol. 6, 231-49.)

Christian morality thus emerges as a response in love to God's initiatives which are mediated primarily through our fellow men. We need not search far and near for God's call, as though the ways of God were unfamiliar to us. The New Testament and theological reflection indicate quite clearly that God's calls lead to the personal service of others as the prime manifestation of faith.

Limitless Love

Life in Christ should manifest the characteristics of the love preached by Jesus. This preaching shows that neighborly concern should not be self-centered, but rather a selfless, disinterested and sacrificial service which recognizes the dignity of other persons. In love, one person offers himself to another in search of unity and the other's welfare. The loved one must be grasped in his personal value, which derives from his uniqueness before God. Personal love recognizes the true autonomy of every individual and never seeks to possess or use a person as one possesses or uses a thing. This serious esteem for all men, even when natural antipathy exists, takes on a new force from the example of Jesus, who loved every man, even sinners, enough to die for them. The love of husband and wife, of mother and child, of friends, provides fleeting images of the immense love which God has manifested to all men in Christ and which he shares in charity. This boundless love moves beyond human limitations, extending even to one's enemies: "You have learned how it was said: You must love your neighbor and hate your enemy. But I say to you: Love your enemies and pray for those who persecute you; in this way you will be sons of your Father in heaven, for he causes his sun to rise on bad men as well as good, and his rain to fall on honest and dishonest men alike. For if you love those who love you, what right have you to claim any credit? Even the tax collectors do as much, do they not? And if you save your greetings for your brothers, are you doing anything exceptional? Even the pagans do as much, do they not? You must therefore be perfect just as your heavenly Father is perfect" (Matt. 5:43-48).

This love must not remain notional, abstract and unreal; it should become embodied in concrete activity. Care, service, concern, marked by the gift of oneself, should characterize the person who professes to follow Christ. The poor, the needy, the neglected, the hungry, the sick, the homeless, the underprivileged of all kinds call for the active intervention of Jesus' disciples. Jesus' own account of the final judgment makes this abundantly clear (Matt. 25:31-46), as do parables such as that of the Good Samaritan (Luke 10:29-37). When entertaining, for example, we should not invite our friends, our brothers, or rich neighbors, but "invite the poor, the crippled, the lame, the blind; that they cannot pay you back means that you are fortunate, because repayment will be made to you when the virtuous rise again" (Luke 14:13-14). Christian charity takes its model in Christ himself, who did not come to be served but to serve, and to surrender his life as a ransom for many (cf. Mark 10:45). St. Paul extolled this active service and concern for others: "If one member suffers anything, all the members suffer with it, or if one member glories, all the members rejoice with it" (1 Cor. 12:26). The callous attitude expressed so tersely in the words "Am I my brother's keeper?" must appear foreign to the person living the life of charity. The promotion of the welfare of other people becomes the true Christian's personal concern. He makes his own the task of fostering the good of others, moving outside his own self-centered circle in disinterested self-giving.

Man in Community

This essential role of the neighbor in Christian morality rules out an individualistic ethic, as though the I-Thou relationship implied in the call-response structure of Christian life concentrated exclusively on the I, to the exclusion of man's social relationships. Man is social in his very roots. In every dimension of his being and in the new kingdom of love, man lives in community and finds God in community. Every I-Thou relationship with God becomes ultimately a we-Thou relationship. Man goes to God with the neighbor and through the neighbor, for he lives as an individual who shares the common bonds of human nature and as a son of the Father called to intimate communion with other men under Christ the head. He loves God and he attains God only through the neighbor, for the neighbor renders God accessible to us as a person in an explicit fashion. It follows that social ethics must constitute a major part of Christian moral theology. War, peace, the racial question, social imbalances of all kinds, cannot simply remain on the periphery of the Christian's moral reflections. Love of the neighbor will carry an authentic concern for man wherever he is found and whatever his problems. Such love is for St. Paul the fulfillment of the law (Rom. 13:8, 10; Gal. 5:14), the bond of perfection (Col. 3:14), and simply the Christian way of life (1 Cor. 12:31-13:13).

7. Virtues, Norms and the Great Commandment

The central importance of charity in the Christian life finds expression frequently under the notion of the primacy of charity in relation to other virtues and all moral norms. The commandment "You shall love your neighbor as yourself" has, in fact, become the starting point for much of the contemporary debate on the renewal of moral theology and on the New Morality. In the following pages, we shall focus on the various ways in which the primacy of charity, especially love of the neighbor, can be understood in moral theology. In succeeding chapters, we shall examine some principal approaches in theological ethics to the problem of specifying and knowing the implications of love.

CHARITY AND THE OTHER VIRTUES

Man realizes himself as a person only in the world of persons through his various activities which incarnate human values. All values and virtues take on their deepest meaning when viewed in their role of promoting the good of other persons and directing the individual toward God, the supreme Value. Truth, justice, chastity, and other particular moral values and virtues serve and respect the neighbor in his profound dignity and uniqueness. They serve as the tangible means whereby man moves through his free choices from the indetermination within the self into the visible world. Man's complex makeup as a spiritual-material creature seeks expression by his multiple powers or faculties of action which translate into practice the richness and dynamism of charity. Charity is man's supreme personal activity and directive force animating other values and virtues. It alone opens man to the whole of reality by directing him to personal union with God and the neighbor. More than attracting man to any particular value or ideal such as do the other virtues, charity attracts man to the fullness of Value and the total Ideal, God himself as Father. Every virtue may thus be seen as a means or a specific end to the ultimate goal of charity. Love is the "radical dynamism" which penetrates into virtues, values and human acts.

The medieval synthesis of St. Thomas Aquinas recognized this unique role of charity by calling it the mother, basis, root and form of all the virtues. Charity alone relates a person to God and to his fellow men in a unifying fashion, and therefore it holds a primacy over other virtues. Gérard Gilleman expresses the same doctrine in stating that every virtue mediates or communicates charity in different dimensions of human existence. Virtue effectively shares in charity; the latter is its origin, animating power, and its sense. (See G. Gilleman, *The Primacy of Charity in Moral Theology,* especially chap. III; E. McDonagh, "The Primacy of Charity," in *Moral Theology Renewed,* 144-49.)

This doctrine of St. Thomas as interpreted by Gilleman expresses accurately the governing and directing force of charity in regard to all Christian virtue worthy of the name. All Christian values and virtues realize and express charity, if they are truly full acts of any particular virtue. For a person to be truthful, just, or chaste without Christian charity lacks the inner vitalizing element which unites the person to his Father in Christ. The outer conduct is devoid of its salvific force.

Emphasis on this understanding of the primacy of charity should serve as a corrective for some notable deficiencies in past moral theology. For example, in some classical presentations of the treatise "On Justice and Rights" (*De jure et justitia*), one reads statements such as the following: "In following this proposed mode of conduct, a person will most likely not violate justice, but he will probably sin against charity, e.g., toward his family," or "one sins only against charity." The implication can easily be given that the "real morality" at stake is the justice obligation; charity may seem a superfluous virtue for the considerations at hand. In a renewed approach to such matters, it does not suffice simply to give a warning at the beginning of the treatment about the narrow perspective employed. Realities of justice, truthfulness, or fidelity should be discussed as they arise in the concrete. If certain actions nearly always violate Christian charity concretely, this should be emphasized. This implies that the proposed action is concretely immoral, for it violates the due love of God and the neighbor, even though the more narrow meaning of justice or another particular virtue is not violated.

Another example may clarify this point. Some explanations of the spouses' mutual availability for sexual relations take on an overly juridical tone, as though only abstract rights and obligations of justice concerning the *debitum* were involved. This tendency bypasses the fullness of the human reality of sexual encounter and prescinds from the emotional, psychological, and bodily factors which constitute the existing person. It may view the husband or wife as "a brain on stilts," without recognizing the other dimensions of non-intellectual life essential to all human activity. Sexuality thus becomes dehumanized. Violations of charity may readily occur simply because the normal sensitivity of one spouse is disregarded. Factors such as time, physical tiredness, psychological readiness and the partner's emotional state will specify the concrete morality of seeking marital relations at a given time. Awareness of these factors implies an openness to the real demands of Christian charity which transcend considerations of the "marital debt," juridically understood. (See J. Bird-L. Bird, *The Freedom of Sexual Love* [Garden City, N.Y.: Doubleday, 1967].)

CHARITY AND MORAL NORMS

Catholic moral theologians and the magisterium of the Church have traditionally accepted the possibility of formulating certain traits or concrete conduct as compatible or not with Christian charity. Love and other virtues form one vast organism of objective congruence with another. To say, for example, that a person fails against justice by stealing also implies his failure in Christian love. Conversely, Christian love can never justify stealing in the proper meaning of the term: taking another's property despite his reasonable unwillingness. Similarly, fornication, adultery, murder, rape and many other modes of specific conduct have been viewed as human activities which embody traits, motives, contravention of duty, and the like which cannot serve as expressions of Christian love. Such acts are incompatible with Christian love, it has been claimed, and are absolutely forbidden.

The ethical system called natural law has been utilized to provide the philosophical and theological underpinnings for this doctrine about what love means. Catholics have maintained on the basis of natural law insights the existence of absolute, universal, negative moral norms. The call of charity does not override such prohibitions; the true dynamism of Christian love cannot seek expression by contravening an accurately formulated moral norm. The encyclical *Humanae Vitae* provides an example of this moral reasoning: "The Church, calling men back to the observance of the norms of the natural law, as interpreted by her constant doctrine, teaches that each and every marriage act must remain open to the transmission of life" (n. 11). "A reciprocal act of love, which jeopardizes the disponibility to transmit life which God the Creator, according to particular laws, inserted therein, is in contradiction with the design constitutive of marriage, and with the will of the Author of life" (n. 13). This highly controverted papal statement asserts that the prohibition of contraception and sterilizing techniques makes an absolute claim on every Christian conscience in forbidding such interventions. The moral norm governing contraception is thus seen as absolute, universal and negative.

Other teachings on specific issues could be cited as additional examples of conduct viewed as incompatible with God's design and, therefore, with Christian love: rape, therapeutic abortion, artificial insemination by a donor, euthanasia, counter-city ABC warfare, pre-marital relations. In each of these type-cases, the formulation of the moral norm governing the area of human activity is interpreted as an accurate summation of the Christian love-response to value in the situation. Christian love cannot realize itself through rape, which violates the dignity and personal integrity of another person; nor through therapeutic abortion, euthanasia, or counter-city ABC warfare, for these fail to respect the human life of other persons which forms the a priori condition of properly loving him; nor through artificial insemination by a donor or through pre-marital relations, for these actions deny the covenantal meaning of Christian marriage between two fully committed spouses.

Christian love has its own meaning, Catholics have taught, and this significance excludes certain actions in every conceivable circumstance. To claim otherwise seems to make love meaningless. "If, for example, 'rape' or 'cruelty to children,' carefully defined of course, could be regarded as expressions of love in some conceivable circumstances, love loses all meaning. If they could not, then there are some absolutes in the Christian ethic, some activities absolutely forbidden, some limits to the behavior which can be an expression of love. Genuine Christian love then demands avoidance of such behavior. Virtues and vices, commands and prohibitions, retain their reality under the primacy of love" (E. McDonagh, "The Primacy of Charity," in *Moral Theology Renewed,* 146).

This traditional Catholic teaching has long been opposed by many Protestant moralists for a variety of theological reasons. Men like Karl Barth, Emil Brunner, and Dietrich Bonhoeffer stress the divine sovereignty whereby God's command in the present moment transcends any normative formulation of obedience. Even biblical injunctions such as the Ten Commandments and the Sermon on the Mount provide unsystematized paradigms or examples of the infinitely varied life of love. They do not, however, offer the Christian a generalized rule for his conduct in anticipation of his particular unique decisions. Other Protestant writers, such as Reinhold Niebuhr, see the doctrine of sin as implying the necessity of compromise because the world of persons and things concretely involves the pervasive presence of conflict and cultural conditioning never fully reconcilable with love. (See G. Outka, "The New Morality: Recent Discussion Within Protestantism," in *The Future of Ethics and Moral Theology,* R. McCormick *et al.,* 44-77, esp. 53-59; J. Milhaven-D. Casey, "Introduction to the Theological Background of the New Morality," *Theological Studies* 28 [1967] 213-44.)

Besides these properly theological reasons for absolutes in

Christian moral doctrine, other factors of contemporary life have recently brought pressure to bear against the traditional Catholic position. The changed world view mentioned previously comes into play in this context. Rather than stressing orderliness, immobility and pre-set moral patterns for conduct, secular and Christian ethicians prefer a view of man and the world which lays its emphasis on change, the freedom of the self to assume responsibility in his unique situation, and the individual character of moral striving. The personal, subjective vision of human action receives a primacy over the historic notion of "man as man," considered in his essential human nature. Attitudes, intentions, and traits—the inner sphere of moral accountability—receive more attention than the external conduct which embodies these interior states.

In 1952, Pope Pius XII condemned a movement which he termed the "new morality," "situation ethics" (Situationsethik), "ethical existentialism," "ethical actualism," and "ethical individualism." He described this movement as follows: "The distinctive mark of this morality is that it is not based in effect on universal moral laws, such as, for example, the Ten Commandments, but on the real and concrete conditions or circumstances in which men must act, and according to which the conscience of the individual must judge and choose. Such a state of things is unique, and is applicable only once for every human action. That is why the decision of conscience, as the advocates of this ethic assert, cannot be commanded by ideas, principles and universal laws" (AAS 44 [1952] 413; see J. Ford-G. Kelly, Contemporary Moral Theology, Vol. I, chap. 7 and 8). The Pope constructed an either-or choice: either universal moral laws exist, or else one accepts the uniqueness of every situation subjectively judged by a person's conscience as the fully decisive moral authority. Pius XII quite definitely committed his authority to the first term of this disjunctive. Catholic moralists in the 1950's and early 1960's devoted most of their endeavors in this context to showing the firm basis of the papal position. (See as examples, R. Gleason, "Situational Morality," Thought 32 [1957] 533-58; A. Carr, "The Morality of Situation Ethics," CTSA Proceedings 12 [1957] 75-102.)

In recent years, the trend of ethical thinking evidenced in Protestant moral theology and in secular ethics has found adherents in Catholic circles. A true *Storm in Ethics* (to use the title of a book on this subject published in 1967) now exists in the Christian Churches of all denominations including the Catholic Church. The question of the New Morality is on everyone's lips, whatever be the name used for it. Polarizing terms frequently recur in the literature: natural law vs. situation ethics, principles vs. contextualism, objectivism vs. subjectivism. It has consequently become increasingly difficult to categorize the disputants so neatly. It even appears necessary at times to deny the accuracy of such nomenclature, especially when one tries to assign a given author to a specific category. James Gustafson has shown well, for instance, how the umbrellas of contextualism and principles have become so sprawling that they include thinkers whose views are as significantly different from each other as they are from persons gathered under the other umbrella. (See his influential article, "Context versus Principles: A Misplaced Debate in Christian Ethics," *Harvard Theological Review* 58 [1965] 171-202; also his "Christian Ethics," in *Religion,* ed. P. Munsey [Englewood Cliffs: Prentice-Hall, 1965] 287-354.) On the other hand, Louis Dupre upholds the continuing relevancy and necessity of the distinction between situation ethics and objective morality, when properly understood, even while calling for "a theory that combines the subjective-creative with the objective-rational element of freedom" (L. Dupre, "Situation Ethics and Objective Morality," *Theological Studies* 28 [1967] 245-57, at 256). Recent writings of Charles Curran also indicate the dangers inherent in assigning an univocal meaning to the notion "natural law." His defense of an updated version of natural law definitely leaves him at odds with many proponents of a "natural law" which differs significantly from his version. (Curran has written chapters on this topic in several books: *Christian Morality Today, A New Look at Christian Morality,* and *Absolutes in Moral Theology?* See also his contribution in G. Outka-P. Ramsey, *Norm and Context in Christian Ethics.*)

THE CONTEXT OF THE CONTEMPORARY DEBATE

The following pages will explore the emerging lines of this debate within Catholicism and within the entire Christian tradition by examining some contemporary attempts to renew the natural law tradition, to introduce insights gained from existential phenomenology and personalism, and to incorporate some valid theological views of other Christians. Before entering the heart of the discussion itself, however, some clarifying reference points may serve to situate better the diverse positions of given authors by providing a broader context.

William K. Frankena, an ethician at the University of Michigan, has formulated several options available to Christian moralists today when they treat this issue of the relation between agape and moral rules. These options depend on the possible sorts of authority which more specific principles and rules may possess in relation to and on the basis of Christian charity or agape. He distinguishes the following options:

"(1) Such rules may be bypassed altogether. All of them may be regarded as unhelpful or clear barriers to personal freedom and 'authenticity.'

(2) They may be taken seriously as useful summaries of past cumulative wisdom, to be set aside whenever love appears to dictate something else in the particular situation.

(3) They may possess general or universal applicability.

(4) There may be combinations of the above" (G. Outka, "The New Morality: Recent Discussion Within Protestantism," in *The Future of Ethics and Moral Theology*, R. McCormick *et al.*, 46).

These four options presented by Frankena relate to a more general position taken by many Christian ethicians who hold that the "law of love" is the sole basis of morality. He calls this position "pure agapism" and describes it as follows: "The rest of the moral law can and must be derived from love together with relevant non-ethical beliefs and knowledge, empirical, metaphysical, or theological" (W. Frankena, "Love and Principle in Christian Ethics," in *Faith and Philosophy*, ed. A. Plantinga [Grand Rapids: W. Eerdmans, 1964] 203-225, at 211). He contrasts this position with "pure non-agapistic theories," that is, those theories which "hold that *all* of the basic judgments of morality proper, whether these are particular or general, are independent of any 'law of love'—that any such law of love, if it is valid at all, is neither necessary nor helpful in morality, and, in fact, does not belong to morality at all" (*ibid.*, 215). This second position no longer has adherents in contemporary Christian ethics. Finally, a third position, termed by Frankena "impure or mixed agapisms," holds the following: "For them there is only one morality by which we are to live but it has two parts. One of its parts is the 'law of love,' the other consists of judgments about right and wrong which are independent of the 'law of love,' judgments which may be either general (rules) or particular. It should be noted here that saying these judgments are independent of the 'law of love' means only that they are not derivative from the 'law of love' in any such way as agapists think they are; it does not mean that they are knowable apart from revelation, grace, or religion" (*ibid.*, 216).

Frankena states that St. Thomas Aquinas, with his emphasis on natural law, pretty clearly holds this third position, whereby the "law of love" and natural law may be viewed as two distinct sources of moral judgments. Frankena seems mistaken in this interpretation, for St. Thomas and contemporary natural law proponents view Christian morality as one whole summed up in Christian charity, agape, "the law of love." (This appears also to be the conclusion of G. Gilleman in *The Primacy of Charity in Moral Theology,* who adheres to St. Thomas' teaching, and of Josef Fuchs in his *Natural Law: A Theological Investigation* 138-43, 164-71.) Frankena's remarks about "pure agapism" can, therefore, serve as a context within which even natural law ethics should be located.

Frankena's technical description of the four options provides further insight into the possible relations existing between moral norms and Christian love.

(1) The most extreme form of pure agapism is *pure act-agapism.* Frankena gives the following description:

This admits no rules or principles other than the "law of love" itself, and it also does not allow that there are any "perceptual intuitions" about what is right or wrong in particular situations independently of the dictates of love. It insists that one is to discover or decide what one's right or duty in a particular situation is solely by confronting one's loving will with the facts about that situation, whether one is an individual or a group. Facts about other situations and ethical conclusions arrived at in other situations are, for this extreme view, simply irrelevant, if not misleading. It adopts with complete literalness, as the whole story, St. Augustine's dictum, "Love, and do as you please." Here belong at least the more drastic of the views sometimes referred to as antinomian, nominalist, existentialist, situationalist, simplistic, or contextualist (*ibid.,* 211).

Catholic moralists have often assumed that the situation ethics condemned by Pope Pius XII fits under this sort of description. The fear exists that such an ethical outlook leads inevitably to relativism and moral arbitrariness, for it assumes a radical discontinuity between discrete moral situations. A unique, ineffable, once-for-ever moment or "situation" seems always to face the moral agent. In such a situation, which is often insufficiently described, the person should do "the loving thing." Love itself will discern its object, without recourse to moral rules. Joseph Fletcher has been accused of holding pure act-agapism, for he constantly stresses the unique and unrepeatable features in each moral situation. (See P. Ramsey's extended criticisms of Fletcher in *Deeds and Rules in Christian Ethics* [N.Y.: C. Scribner's, 1967] 145-240.) Fletcher has explicitly denied that he holds this theory in his work *Situation Ethics* (Philadelphia: Westminster, 1966); he prefers to term his version of situation ethics "modified rule-agapism. It is to be noted, of course, that my method stresses the act (that is, the act-in-the situation), whereas Ramsey's stresses the 'principles' or moral generalizations and value propositions which are called into play and reference" (*Storm Over Ethics,* J. Bennett *et al.,* 157). Fletcher contends that he holds Frankena's second form of pure agapism: "summary rule agapism," which we shall now treat.

Frankena gives the following introduction to options other than pure act-agapism: "The other forms of pure agapism all take rules or principles to be necessary or at least helpful in guiding the loving Christian individual (or group) in the determination of his (its) rights and duties in particular cases. But, being forms of pure agapism, they regard all such rules or principles as somehow derivative from love" (*ibid.*, 212).

(2) The second option given by Frankena is *summary rule* or *modified act-agapism* (Fletcher prefers to call this "modified rule-agapism").

> This admits rules but regards them as summaries of past experience, useful, perhaps almost indispensable, but only as rules of thumb. It cannot allow that a rule may ever be followed in a situation when it is seen to conflict with what love dictates in that situation. For, if rules are to be followed only insofar as they are helpful as aids to love, they cannot constrain or constrict love in any way. But they may and perhaps should be used" (*ibid.*, 212).

Frankena believes that some contextualists or "circumstance" moralists fit under this heading, though he cites only Joseph Sittler (*The Structure of Christian Ethics*). The two most prominent exponents of situation ethics on a popular level in the English-speaking world, Joseph Fletcher and Bishop John A. T. Robinson (*Honest to God* [London: SCM, 1963]; *Christian Morals Today* [London: SCM, 1964]), also profess this second option. For these authors, the proper way to state moral rules is to say, for example, "Keeping promises is generally love-fulfilling." Such rules, Fletcher claims, should be understood as illuminative maxims rather than directive precepts (*Situation Ethics,* 31). They have validity solely as "statistically preponderant generalizations." Though they usually apply to moral situations, they may never be followed in a particular situation when following them is known not to have the most love-fulfilling consequences in this particular case (Frankena, 208). General moral principles, norms, or rules illuminate a situation as guidelines, but without necessarily predetermining one's action. Fletcher calls this view a "principled relativism" (*Storm Over Ethics,* 156). No moral rule can, therefore, claim an absolute or universal validity.

Fletcher succinctly describes his view as follows:

> Situationism holds, on the one hand, that rules are not ab-
> solutely or universally valid, thus modifying legalism. At the
> same time it modifies the unprincipledness of extemporism by
> holding that general principles in normative ethics may some-
> times, even often, be relevant and obliging because they hap-
> pen to be consistent in concrete situations with the trans-
> normative criterion or formal imperative. For Christians this
> criterion is agape (J. Fletcher, "What's in a Rule?: A Situa-
> tionist's View," in *Norm and Context in Christian Ethics,* ed.
> G. Outka-P. Ramsey, 325-49, at 332).

Robinson proposes also this notion of summary rules:

> What "love's casuistry" requires makes . . . the most search-
> ing demands both upon the depth and integrity of one's con-
> cern for the other . . . and upon the calculation of what is
> truly the most loving thing in this situation for every person
> involved. Such an ethic cannot but rely, in deep humility,
> upon guiding rules, upon the cumulative experience of one's
> own and other people's obedience. It is this bank of experi-
> ence which gives us our working rules of "right" and "wrong"
> and without them we could not but flounder (J. Robinson,
> *Honest to God,* 119-20; see also his *Christian Morals Today,*
> esp. chap. 1).

These summary rules or illuminative maxims have no ontological basis, according to Fletcher. Casting aside the extremes
of what he terms antinomianism (no law whatsoever) and
legalism (absolute and universal laws prevail in morals), he ex-
pounds "a new, serious, and deliberate relativism," which entails
a modern nominalism. "Goodness is extrinsic, not intrinsic in
human acts." The Catholic natural law position and the scriptural
law tradition of classical Protestant theology stand explicitly re-
pudiated by this outlook. (See *Norm and Context in Christian
Ethics,* 333-34.) The particular situation of individual persons
and the specific consequences of one's act occupy the center of
attention. The individual person must decide in each situation
whether the summary rule or maxim in question will serve love
then and there, and if not, disregard it. These rules are estab-

lished inductively from experience, and if the person's here-and-now experience indicates that more good consequences can be effected in some other way, then the rule at issue should be suspended, ignored, or violated. For Fletcher, this understanding holds true even for the Ten Commandments:

> The one universal requirement is to love others, God and men, as ourselves. Anything else, including those ancient theophanic-nomadic rules called the Ten Commandments, are *relatively* valid—relative to any situation in which their meaning might happen to be fitting to love's requirements. Only love is absolute, and it is this anchorage which makes it possible for situationism's relativization of all rules to be genuinely relativistic, and not merely chaotic and random and sheerly unrelated (*Norm and Context in Christian Ethics*, 335).

Paul Ramsey has analyzed Fletcher's ethical position at great length in his *Deeds and Rules in Christian Ethics* (145-240). Perhaps his most telling criticism denies Fletcher's contention about his personal position: "In actual fact Fletcher's operating ethical method is an extreme and exclusive act-agapism; if not *anti*nomian, it is certainly *anomia* (lawless), no matter how he formally defines situation ethics and attempts to locate it in between extremes" (*ibid.*, 148). On the other hand, Ramsey sees Robinson's view of morality as tending logically toward the acceptance of some absolute rules, that is, toward Frankena's third option of "pure rule-agapism." Gene Outka has recently given a good summary of Ramsey's various comments on Fletcher and Robinson. Since these Protestant moralists have so prominent a place in the current debate about law and love, Outka's remarks about their adherence to the summary rule position are reproduced here in full:

> The summary rule position, in and of itself, he takes to be fundamentally an unstable one. One of its major defenders, Fletcher, is constantly inclined de facto to stress the unique and unrepeatable features in each situation, whereas another defender, Robinson, emphasizes the need for "working rules" to such an extent that they appear rather unambiguously general in their binding character. Such instability is due on the one side, Ramsey holds, to the logical priority which the

particular case invariably retains in relation to any summary rule. Certainly the situationist is prepared to admit that many such rules may be practically indispensable in helping us to expedite the routine matters of daily existence. But they are not formally indispensable in any way. They may always be ignored or discarded and they are not (even) assumed to be relevant prior to the situation, nor does allowing them to be overriden bear a special burden of proof. Whether the situationist "follows or violates a summary rule or principle, he still goes about deciding in that act of self-elected sovereignty, by a direct application of agape to that particular case, what is the right thing to do. . . ."

Ramsey does not mean to deny that a great part of the moral life is appropriately governed by a direct appeal to love and the illumination furnished by summary rules. What he rejects is the claim that the only legitimate use of rules is as maxims or summaries of past experience. This claim cannot do justice to a host of factors, including (1) the rules of social practice, (2) an adequate philosophy of law, (3) a comprehensive doctrine of justice and human rights, and (4) a minimally probing view of "the convenants of life with life."

The instability of summary rule agapism likewise is manifested in the tendency toward general rules of some of its exponents. Though Ramsey has Robinson mainly in mind in this regard, he does point out that, in an earlier book on the ethics of medical practice, Fletcher himself defended as a general rule "the patient's right to know the truth." The right was "not a conclusion that awaits, or would vary according to the particularities of, an individual medical or personal diagnosis." Ramsey argues that the defense of this general rule is quite inconsistent with Fletcher's subsequent views, but it nicely illustrates the instability. "One quite general rule would be quite sufficient to subvert the exclusive claims of situation ethics" (G. Outka in *The Future of Ethics and Moral Theology,* R. McCormick *et al.,* 62-63).

This extended treatment of summary rule agapism may give insight into the contemporary tendency to confer a logical sovereignty on love in relation to moral norms. Love decides anew in the concrete situation whether these summary rules or illuminative maxims should be given moral weight. Ramsey has noted some important reservations about this option, especially as found in Fletcher's writings. Other reservations could be added: What does "love" really mean for Fletcher? "Love people, not

principles," he says. But the question remains: How does one
really love? Gustafson has stated in seeming exasperation:

> "Love" like "situation" is a word that runs through Fletcher's
> book like a greased pig. . . . Nowhere does Fletcher indicate
> in a systematic way his various uses of it. It refers to every-
> thing he wants it to refer to. It is the *only* thing that it
> intrinsically good; it equals justice; it is a formal *principle;*
> it is a *disposition,* it is a predicate and not a property, it is a
> ruling norm (J. Gustafson, "Love Monism," in *Storm Over
> Ethics,* 33).

How does one determine the loving thing? Following summary
rule agapism alone, for example, one might well hold that adultery is generally wrong, but at times it might be the loving thing
to do. (See Fletcher's famous example in *Situation Ethics,*
165.) On the other hand, is it possible to characterize some
classes of human acts as having clear, intrinsic and irreducible
human and Christian significance which connotes a moral significance attached to the proposed conduct? Are there any actions
which *as such* are loving or unloving? (See R. McCormick, "Contextualism vs. Principles," *Theological Studies* 27 [1966] 610-20,
esp. 613-16.) Catholic moral theologians in the main hold that
there exist other moral rules or principles than so-called summary
rules. In this they part ways with Fletcher and situationists in
general, arriving at the final two options offered by Frankena.

(3) Frankena terms the third option *pure rule-agapism.* His
description follows:

> It maintains that we are always to tell what we are to do in
> particular situations by referring to a set of rules, and that
> what rules are to prevail and be followed is to be determined
> by seeing what rules (not what acts) best or most fully em-
> body love (*ibid.,* 212).

For pure rule-agapism the proper way to state a moral
rule is, for example, "Keeping-promises-always is love-fulfilling." This principle has a general validity and its violation
could never express love or be love-fulfilling. Frankena claims
that according to pure rule-agapism "we may and sometimes
must obey a rule in a particular situation even though the
action it calls for is seen not to be what love itself would

directly require. For pure rule-agapism, in other words, the rules may in a sense constrict the direct expression of love" (*ibid.*, 212-13).

Ramsey rightly contends that this latter statement of Frankena's prejudices the discussion about rules from the very beginning, "if pure rule-agapism is defined in such fashion that this means that a Christian should obey a rule 'even though the action it calls for is seen not to be what love itself would directly require.' That would be to do less or something other than love requires" (*Deeds and Rules in Christian Ethics,* 111). The pure rule-agapist holds for more than summary rules, but these always-binding rules embody love. Starting with persons, not with the rules themselves, the Christian asks: What does love require? If some general principles, or rules, or virtues, or styles of life have a general validity as embodying love, then pure rule-agapism has a basis. Rigorous logic leads in fact to Ramsey's view: "A single exception to act-agapism and to summary rule-agapism would be sufficient to destroy these positions utterly and to establish general rule-agapism in at least some types of actions" (*ibid.,* 129). Catholic moralists and the magisterium of the Church have claimed that numerous general rules exist, for example, rape, therapeutic abortion, artificial insemination by a donor, euthanasia, counter-city ABC warfare, pre-marital relations. Ramsey also cites examples of general rules which embody loving traits and conduct:

Answers that have been given to this question include the characteristics of love peerlessly set forth in 1 Corinthians 13 (which are all, so far as I can see, universal statements about what agape requires); the qualities called the "fruits," and "Beatitudes" in Thomistic ethics; what Christ teaches us concerning the broadest and deepest meaning of justice; the bond of marriage tempered to the meaning and strength indicated in Ephesians 5; order, or the orders, in dialectical relation with justice and with love; truth-telling and promise-keeping; and (as the floor below which love cannot and may not and must not fall) those works of sin in the flesh listed in Scripture, the more or less than seven more or less deadly sins, or those "classes of things" like murder, theft, rape, promiscuity, pillage, adultery, and sexual relations that are genuinely and therefore irresponsibly pre-marital. Some of these things may not be quite general, and there may be more to be added that will always and everywhere form the conscience and the life of the Christian man (*Deeds and Rules in Christian Ethics,* 112-13).

Outka believes that in this listing of general rules, Ramsey "seems more convincing in adducing standards and relations than classes of external behavior" (*The Future of Ethics and Moral Theology,* 72). For example, Outka has less difficulty in holding to the unexceptionableness of patience or kindness than of theft. The Catholic natural law tradition and Ramsey himself adhere, nevertheless, to the possibility of adequately formulated, general rules for some moral choices. These general rules have been seen to arise from the requirements of love in particular experienced actions. These rules embody love's penetration to the full meaning of human persons and to the past consequences of service to the neighbor in similar circumstances. No possible genuine exception to the general rule seems logically or realistically possible. Action in accord with the principle, it is contended, will always be the most love-fulfilling act in similar situations. General rule-agapism, therefore, begins with persons and discerns some rules expressing love which have a general validity. The norm embodies and enshrines an underlying value of importance to man.

Past tendencies in Catholic moral theology have led to an over-extension of such general rules. An exaggerated casuistry reduced morality to a handy catalogue of determined, conceptualized norms, applicable in all situations. Current effects to update moral theology, however, show reactive tendencies in the opposite direction, that is, toward pure act-agapism or summary rule-agapism. In this situation, a balanced approach is needed, but difficult to maintain.

(4) The fourth form of pure agapism mentioned by Frankena involves combinations of act-agapism and rule-agapism:

Here would fall, for instance, the view that, while we may and should appeal to rules when we can in deciding what should be done in a particular case, as the rule-agapist holds, we may and should appeal to the "law of love" directly in

cases for which there are no rules or in which the rules conflict, just as the act-agapist does. Such combinations may, in
fact, be more plausible than either pure act-agapism or pure
rule-agapism by themselves (*ibid.*, 214).

This view holds the possibility, then, of a variety of situations
and moral problems. The direct appeal to love should be made
in some instances; at other times, summary rules may assist in
reaching a moral verdict; or a general moral rule may simply
find immediate application. At the least, moral rules have some
relevance in reaching judgments. Unlike pure act-agapism as the
sole governing theory, the person does not simply determine then
and there in each situation what is "the loving thing." Ramsey
finds this option quite attractive: "It would seem, in fact, that
if a Christian ethicist is going to be a pure agapist he would find
this fourth possibility to be the most fruitful one, and most in
accord with the freedom of agape both to act through the firm-
est principles and to act, if need be, without them" (*Deeds and
Rules in Christian Ethics,* 107). It should be noted, however, that
in holding this fourth option, Ramsey defends the real possibility
of unexceptionable general rules, such as in the third option. (See
P. Ramsey, "The Case of the Curious Exception," in *Norm and
Context in Christian Ethics,* ed. G. Outka-P. Ramsey, 67-135.)
In this, he differs from Gene Outka, who interprets this fourth
option as envisioning some rules which are "always relevant in
any situation to which it is applicable, but not invariably decisive.
This is approximately the 'combinationist' view. Certain rules
have such authority . . . that they are never disregarded but
only overridden" (G. Outka, *The Future of Ethics and Moral
Theology,* 70). He cites the rule prohibiting adultery as an example of such a rule.

This final option seems acceptable, if taken in a sense which
truly allows the existence of some general moral rules in addition
to so-called summary rules. As will be argued in the following
chapter, there exist solid reasons to uphold man's possibility of
formulating norms which state what is authentically human in a
variety of situations. We shall discuss the question within the
framework of contemporary thought on natural law.

BIBLIOGRAPHY

Curran, C., "Dialogue with Joseph Fletcher," in *A New Look at Christian Morality* (Notre Dame: Fides, 1968) 159-75.

Dupre, L., "Situation Ethics and Objective Morality," *Theological Studies* 28 (1967) 245-57.

Fletcher, J., *Situation Ethics* (Philadelphia: Westminster, 1966).

————, "Situation Ethics Under Fire," in *Storm Over Ethics*, J. Bennett *et al.* (United Church Press, 1967) 149-73.

————, "What's in a Rule? A Situationist's View," in *Norm and Context in Christian Ethics*, ed. G. Outka-P. Ramsey (N.Y.: C. Scribner's, 1968) 325-49.

Frankena, W., "Love and Principle in Christian Ethics," in *Faith and Philosophy*, ed. A. Plantinga (Grand Rapids: W. Eerdmans, 1964) 203-25. Excerpts used by permission.

McDonagh, E., "The Primacy of Charity," in *Moral Theology Renewed*, ed. E. McDonagh (Dublin: Gill & Son, 1965) 130-50.

Milhaven, J.-Casey, D., "Introduction to the Theological Background of the New Morality," *Theological Studies* 28 (1967) 213-44.

Outka, G., "The New Morality: Recent Discussion within Protestantism," in *The Future of Ethics and Moral Theology*, R. McCormick *et al.* (Chicago: Argus, 1968) 44-77.

Ramsey, P., *Deeds and Rules in Christian Ethics* (N.Y.: C. Scribner's, 1967).

————, "The Case of the Curious Exception," in *Norm and Context in Christian Ethics*, ed. G. Outka-P. Ramsey (N.Y.: C. Scribner's, 1968) 67-135.

Robinson, J., *Christian Morals Today* (London: SCM, 1964).

————, *Honest to God* (London: SCM, 1963).

8. Natural Law in the Christian Life

Contemporary critics have singled out natural law as a prime contributor to the alleged decadence of Catholic moral theology. The negativism, absolutism, and minimalism attributed to moral theology are often traced back to natural law as the root cause. This is termed a medieval, anachronistic system of ethical thought which fails to meet the needs of man in a technological age. The very "naturalness" and "legality" implied in the term natural law have, moreover, led to continued questioning about its place in the Gospel morality. These criticisms seem understandable, if not fully acceptable, because traditional presentations of Catholic morality have natural law as their basis and core content. Dissatisfaction with moral theology inevitably implies dissatisfaction with natural law, and the converse also holds true.

Despite the renewed interest in natural law so evident in Catholic writings since World War II, we may well question the solidity of these convictions among present-day Catholic philosophers and theologians. Natural law is currently under serious attack. Our ecumenical age sees Catholic theologians asking whether the morality of the New Covenant even tolerates the inclusion of, or at least a limited recourse to, a natural law. Similarly, the contraception controversy finds authors wondering why only Catholic Christians seem to have an insight into this point of natural law. They frequently proceed to reconsider the theory and application of natural law and, sometimes, to reject it outright as irrelevant. In light of these sincere inquiries, it seems wrong to claim a rebirth of natural law in current Catholic theology and philosophy, let alone outside the Church. It seems preferable to stress the need for updating and renewing natural law, hopefully leading to a future revitalization of the doctrine. (See G.

Regan, "The Need for Renewal in Natural Law," *The Catholic Lawyer* 12 [1966] 135-40.)

In this chapter, we shall devote our attention to some selected issues in today's debate about natural law. Does natural law accord with the scriptural data? What efficacy does natural law have in the revealed Christian era of salvation? What does the Church teach about natural law and what force does this teaching possess? Finally, what does natural law ultimately mean and what relevence does it have? We shall take up this last question in the first place, for unless one understands the meaning of natural law, it seems impossible to judge about its acceptability within Christian morals.

THE MEANING OF NATURAL LAW

The doctrine of natural law finds rejection in many quarters on the basis of often-repeated distortions of the authentic tradition. The accusations range through abstractionism, intuitionism, legalism, immobilism, and biologism (found frequently in the literature on contraception), to a rationalism which ignores the fullness of intersubjective reality. (See J. Murray, *We Hold These Truths* [N.Y.: Sheed & Ward, 1960] 295-96.) John Courtney Murray, however, has acutely observed that the critics of natural law are forever burying the wrong corpse. Most notable in these caricatures, in the context of current moral theology, are the allegations concerning immobilism and rationalism. These qualifications applied accurately to the 17th—18th-century brand of natural law (iusnaturalism) which has become the standard-bearer in many legal circles for the entire doctrine. This understanding of natural law contended that from such general premises as "do good and avoid evil," or "do unto others as you would have them do unto you," the entire ethical life could be deduced. A true set of foreordained moral principles, a code of natural law, could thus be established. This Age of Reason could confidently assert such bizarre conclusions as the jury system of trial or the international postal system belongs to the natural law. (See M. Crowe, "Natural Law Theory Today," in *The Future of Ethics and Moral Theology,* 83-84.) Such deductionism has few, if any, proponents in the mainstream of Catholic thought today.

What might be described then as natural law? In its essential features, the authentic doctrine states that every man can grasp through his reasoning powers the main ethical implications of his own being taken in all his vital relationships to God, the world, and other persons. Man does not create his own moral norms in an ethical void. Social bodies such as the State do not ultimately determine the rightness and wrongness of human acts. Man's own being serves as the ontological basis for what man should become through his free choices. "Become what you already are," rightly understood, gives a fundamental insight into the root of natural law. Simply stated, the doctrine of natural law holds that man must fashion, guide and enlighten his own ethical life-project by taking due account of the infinitely varied and dynamic possibilities inherent in his unique self. Man becomes a law unto himself in fulfilling the innermost demands of his being toward his authentic self-realization. (See L. Monden, "Legal Ethics or Situation Ethics?" in *Sin, Liberty and Law* [N.Y.: Sheed & Ward, 1965] 73-144.)

"Human nature" signifies the inviting fullness of man's being which charts his ethical becoming. No abstract blueprint or pre-fabricated model of the moral life, human nature instead means the whole of that concrete, existing man called here-and-now to choose morally. This meaning surpasses any merely abstract significance of human nature understood as man's metaphysical being realized in a univocal, immutable and universal way. Man's metaphysical qualities, such as his creaturely dependence on God, his key social relationships, his bisexuality and freedom of choice, belong to every man's inalienable and fundamental being, but they do not found the fullness of man's total being. The "human nature" which should be emphasized in natural law doctrine is instead existing, concrete human nature, which includes all man's being as realized existentially in specific situations. All man's being, including his metaphysical qualities, should be viewed as morally relevant in this understanding of human nature. An individual's temperament, intellectual acumen, race, marital status, biocultural development, professional qualifications, and intersubjective relationships may in a sense be only accidental or non-essential in relation to man's metaphysical being, but they constitute major elements in discerning his proper moral choices. Every facet of his being forms a bundle of dynamic inviting possibilities for that law of self-growth called natural law. To act in accord with every dimension of your being thus constitutes the principal message of natural law doctrine. In free and responsible control of his development, each person becomes in St. Thomas' phrase "his own providence," actively sharing by his foresight and care in the completion of his own self-perfection. (See G. Regan, "Natural Law in the Church Today," *The Catholic Lawyer* 13 [1967] 21-41.)

A few examples may clarify this basic understanding of natural law. Nearly all men become conscious throughout their life-experiences of the existence of an Absolute in their lives which gives sense and direction to their strivings and serves as the fullness of intermediate values and goals. Most men articulate this Absolute as being God himself, the highest Value. Their relation to him unifies their myriad activities and they gradually grasp that their contingent, creaturely status owes its origin and continuing existence to God. Almost intuitively, as a consequence of their experienced understanding of the meaning which God occupies in their lives, men grasp the basic need of due respect to him and the destruction of this relationship connoted by such acts as blasphemy. The personal appropriation of God as Supreme Value sees blasphemy as twisting the very contingent being of man in its inner sense. Blasphemy may be said to go against man's nature. "Thou shalt not blaspheme," or some similar formulation, would accurately state the moral norm arrived at by this self-understanding of man's vital relationship to God. It serves as a negative, limiting guideline, the minimum demanded of every person.

Man's experience of his relationships with other persons also gradually introduces the profound insight that he and every individual possess a unique, irreducible significance and worth which can never be ignored in any free choices. Certain fundamental attitudes stem from this basic recognition of the value of every person: a respect for human life, the acknowledgment of the freedom of others, their inherent right to be treated as conscious and respectable subjects and not as things. Reason discerns that the dignity of other persons should be promoted by the whole web of ongoing relationships that constitute the social life of each individual. To violate the dignity of others rends the relationship itself, for the other finds rejection as a person. Most so-called moral obligations and moral failures occur in the midst of these living relationships to other people. Under a certain point of view, nearly the entire moral life could be construed as the recognition in human action of one's vital relationships to others and the consequent moral duties flowing from this insight. (See X. Colavechio, "Conscience: A Personalist Perspective," *Continuum* 5 [1967] 203-10.)

Once a person arrives at a stage in his self-development where he can grasp personally the inherent dignity of each person, he sees that certain specific human actions, carefully described and lived in human experience, run counter to individual dignity of others, for these actions fail to respect others. The relevant features of some human actions, therefore, cause men to denominate the type-action as immoral. Rape, wanton murder, brainwashing or other invasions of psychic privacy or thought-control, slavery, genocide, and sexual promiscuity have been seen, through individual and communal insights gained by experience, as violations of the very being or dignity of other persons. To ignore the basic datum that, for example, rape intrudes on the freedom and autonomy of a woman in any foreseeable circumstances seems unacceptable. In any conceivable situation, can rape constitute a humanly fulfilling moral choice? Or does it always and necessarily constitute an affront to the dignity of another person? To state that rape is always wrong simply means that as a human reality it has an irreducible significance as violating another person's right to corporal and psychic integrity. (See R. McCormick, "Human Significance and Christian Significance," in *Norm and Context in Christian Ethics,* ed. G. Outka-P. Ramsey, 233-61.)

Natural law thus proposes the charter of a true humanism in moral conduct, for it emphasizes that the whole meaning of man enters as a relevant and ineradicable datum in every moral choice. It emerges as an optimistic understanding about man and his moral life, for it rests on an epistemology which contends that man can intelligently grasp and freely assume the divine call in his regard without recourse to outside, compelling moral norms. The law of his being guides him. In the authentic approach to natural law, moreover, man does not face his being or nature as an order or necessity which he blindly fulfills in a fatalistic manner. Man stands at the summit of all created being as God's chief glory, who has received the divine invitation to serve as architect of the attainment of his destiny. Natural law thus becomes the logical consequence of the philosophico-theological understanding of man as the image of God in his self-transcendence which opens him to the Absolute. The accusations of abstractionism and immobilism fall on hollow ears if one views natural law as elaborating a set of real data based on the living experience of people. (See J. Fuchs, *Human Values and Christian Morality,* 140-47.)

L. Monden has summarized well the basic elements of this approach:

That *inner law of growth* has traditionally borne the name "natural law." Hence in its classical meaning the term "natural law" has *no connection with the physical or biological concept of "nature,"* formerly in frequent use in the positive sciences and in ethics, with which it is often wrongly identified even nowadays (for instance, in the treatment of sexual problems). Thus some actions are supposed to be "according to" or "against" nature. But an action which is biologically "according to" nature may very well be morally in conflict with the "natural law." Hence the fact that the notion of "nature" is outmoded in the positive sciences cannot be used as an argument against the natural law in the moral sense, since it has no connection whatsoever with it. . . . Historically . . . the natural law . . . appealed to an unwritten law, an inborn knowledge of what man ought to do and ought not to do in order to be and to become authentically himself. . . . In its original meaning the natural law is a dynamic existing reality, an ordering of man toward his self-perfection and his self-realization, through all the concrete situations of his life and in intersubjective dialogue with his fellow man and with God. . . . It is precisely man's becoming which is prefigured in it. The norm of man's action is not so much what he is as what he is to become (L. Monden, *Sin, Liberty and Law,* 88-89).

THE FORMULATION OF UNWRITTEN LAW

In its primary sense, the natural law is an unformulated law rooted in man's being. In a secondary and derived sense, however, the natural law becomes formulated into propositions or norms of morality which have a general or universal application. This derived meaning of natural law gives rise to many difficulties in connection with the existence of universal, absolute moral norms. Can man probe the inner significance of his being so as to formulate accurate universal norms which suffer no exception? Or does self-knowledge imply an historical, dynamic process of gradually developing insights into the implications of what it means to be man? How much do factors of man's biocultural development limit the possibilities of formulating norms which bind in any epoch?

These and similar questions are currently debated in the literature on natural law and moral theology in general. Any attempt at a solution to these difficulties must employ some understanding of an epistemology of ethics. (See J. Milhaven, "Toward an Epistemology of Ethics," *Theological Studies* 27 [1966] 228-41; reprinted in G. Outka-P. Ramsey, *Norm and Context in Christian Ethics,* 219-31; R. McCormick cogently questions the sufficiency of Milhaven's statement in his article in the same book, pp. 251f.) The intellectualist tradition flowing through St. Thomas to the present-day natural law schools has defended man's capacity to single out essential structures of his nature which imply unchanging, permanently valid moral imperatives. The tendency has existed to over-extend the number of these universal, absolute norms based on man's metaphysical structures. Such a tendency has led to rather absurd conclusions in past formulations of supposedly absolute principles. This should not, however, deter us from asking whether the basic possibility exists of formulating at least some such principles or norms.

The starting point of this inquiry should be man as he really exists concretely, not some a priori, abstract human nature. In reflecting on existing man or individual persons, one sees that diversity of temperament, intellectual ability, physical characteristics, moral qualities, marital status, sex, and other specific qualifications take on a prominence in our knowledge of this unique individual. The freedom of the human spirit to transcend his environment, to reach out toward the unexpected, enters our consciousness as part of our experience of other persons. Emotions, dislikes, loves, aesthetic awareness and a host of other personality features set off *this* person from all other persons. In comparing groups of people from different nations, cultures or ethnic backgrounds the same diversity or dissimilarity enters our experience. The same holds true when we reflect on the substantial growth which man experiences as he lives out his history in different eras. Is the caveman really man in the same sense as we experience man today? Has the technological and atomic age introduced a substantial, essential change into the meaning of man, taken in any realistic, existing sense?

These cultural, historical, and personal differences and modifications lead many contemporaries to view man as not having a fixed nature. Existentialists will claim that man's nature is not to have a nature, meaning by the term a static, unchangeable given which sets the outer limits for man's exercise of his freedom. The autonomy and self-transcendence of man, not his stable qualities, should receive emphasis. This contemporary outlook implies an actual change in the underlying world-view of man and the universe. Stability, unchangeableness, universality, traditionally viewed as positive notes of perfection, run counter to the dynamism, development, growth processes and constant improvement which characterize man's chosen goals. Contemporary man remains unsatisfied with an understanding of himself and his world which gives him at birth a pre-formulated package of his moral life. He does not view himself as a programmed computer.

An awareness of these criticisms and apprehensions about past views of human nature, however, does not of itself lead to the necessary conclusion that the human consciousness cannot discern any rather stable and permanent features in man viewed ontologically. Does not our experience of real, existing men indicate many universal, common elements in any man? The fact that an older world-view brought these features into too great a prominence and identified man's nature with nearly total immutability, stability, and other universal qualities does not invalidate the possibility of discerning some universal features in people which may have moral implications. To act in accord with or to violate the meaning of these universal features may constitute only a small part of man's moral task, but this part can have enormous importance. These features can address moral obligations to the freedom of the individual. This happens most often in a negative and limiting sense for possible moral choices. That is, in reflecting on man's metaphysical structures, ethics arrives at a minimum boundary below which his authentic freedom cannot descend if he is to act humanly. Most frequently, these insights into the implications of man's being receive a formulation in negative, minimalistic terms, "Thou shalt not. . . ." This connotes that man's dynamic moral life, his life of adventurous response to all his vital relationships, will not find its authentic self-realization in the prohibited area. "Become what you are": but can man fulfill himself by insulting his Creator? Does he respect his own being and the dignity of other persons by freely disposing of his own life or their lives? Does sexual promiscuity or rape accord with the psychosomatic, personalized meaning of human sexuality? Man's insights in these areas of his being should lead to the conclusion that his personal freedom cannot ignore these outstanding structures of his being.

On the basis of such insights gained in personal and collective human experience, it seems feasible to formulate at least some universal, negative and absolute moral norms. The number of these may be rather few compared to traditional listings; their content may be somewhat general and not descend into great detail; but in principle their existence seems legitimate. Man's continued reasonings, whether of individual persons or of the living community, require constant contact with vital experiences, together with exacting inquiry into the impact of ongoing social and historical forces. An abstract, inert view of man will not suffice. These reasonings, moreover, should not be construed as existing on the same level of immediacy or specificity, as far as man's moral perception is concerned. For instance, an outright act of murder performed against an innocent child or adult, without mitigating circumstances, would be universally condemned by mankind. Such moral intuition may simply be looked upon as the common possession of all men. The experience of the value of human life leads immediately to the knowledge of the corresponding moral norm: wanton disregard for human life can, therefore, never be justified. "Thou shalt not murder . . ." would find easy application in all cases, if all killing of human beings were to fit this description. However, the fullness of concrete, existing reality involves far more complications in nearly all instances. When the killing adds circumstances in the moral situation such as "a person sick and dying of cancer," or "an inviable fetus whose mother's life is threatened," or "a pregnancy resulting from rape," or, in some cultures, "an innocent person, but a member of another tribe," man's moral perception of values becomes colored or more clouded. As a result, even ethicians dispute the morality of some cases of euthanasia, therapeutic abortion, a spy's taking of his own life, the treatment of captured enemy soldiers, and other involved realities. The formal, unquestioned statement, "Thou shalt not kill," may be changed to "Thou shalt not murder," but the problem still remains: What morally constitutes murder? To violate the dignity of another person by unjustifiably killing him is immoral; but what makes the act unjustifiable? How does one distinguish euthanasia from the limited duty of preserving one's life? It requires entire moral texts to elaborate the ethical theory behind such important matters as the distinction between direct and indirect killing, the concept of killing an unjust aggressor, capital punishment, counter-city ABC warfare, euthanasia versus the limited duty of preserving human life, and so forth. (See C. Curran, "Absolute Norms and Medical Ethics," in *Absolutes in Moral Theology?*, 108-53.)

These examples point to the fact that at the outer limits of many generally accepted and cogent norms of natural law, there may be lacking necessary evidence or rigor of proof. These borderline areas of moral discernment sometimes introduce a certain grayness into our moral life, despite a normal bent toward black and white choices. Most persons accept unquestioningly a number of rather broad moral principles, but grow hesitant as one specifies concrete moral demands which claim some basis in these principles. The preservation of human life, the promotion of truthfulness and confidence in interpersonal communications, the desire to give each man his due, all seem acceptable as moral attitudes which should apply in any conceivable situation. But specifications such as "therapeutic abortion is always wrong," or "euthanasia is always wrong," or "lying is always wrong," or "stealing, even from large corporations or the government, is always wrong," find at best grudging acceptance in many quarters and outright rejection among some ethicians. The honest question is asked whether these moral norms enshrine or protect unchanging and unexceptionable human values which possess permanent significance in every situation.

Some human reasonings and insights, we may suppose, may well express only indications, recommendations, or generally desirable goals, but do not have their foundation in absolute, unchanging features of man or his moral actions. A major challenge faced by natural law adherents today above all is the need to reexamine many traditionally held universal, negative, absolute formulations and honestly ask whether they can be sustained as necessary implications of man's existing human nature. St. Thomas himself explicitly envisaged possible failures in formulating more detailed requirements of natural law, the so-called secondary precepts of natural law, and traced them back to man's inability at times to reason properly, as well as to the effect of emotional involvement in the concrete situation, to lack of cultural development of individuals or of a society, and simply to bad habits. (See Crowe, 96-99.) Progress in man's moral perceptions has occurred in such matters as religious liberty, slavery, usury, the use of torture to exact confessions, and, in the judgment of many, responsible parenthood. What does man's being demand today? This question must be faced anew in light of our contemporary view of human existence and developments in the world of everyday reality. Some past formulations of the unwritten law of man's being may fall by the wayside. Fresh insights may give rise to new moral claims as consistent with man's historical consciousness. Might this already be the case in issues involving capital punishment, selective conscientious objection, or racial equality? Possible changes in cherished formulations of moral norms should not cut off inquiry. To risk need not mean to err.

On the other hand, the intricacy of the moral life should not be overly exaggerated, as though every day brought each individual a string of totally unrepeatable and unique moral choices. A theory of radical discontinuity or dissimilarity in moral situations does not mirror reality. People simply do not face startling moral dilemmas day in and day out. J. Fletcher cites conflict-of-duty cases with such frequency that his moral theology consists practically of an ethics of the exceptional instance, though his analysis lacks a coherent foundation. Experience dictates instead that the same morally relevant features occur repeatedly in choices entering the lives of different people. These relevant features of the given situation seem uncompromisable and must always be seriously weighed. For example, though every person's suffering and death be unique, unrepeatable, ineffable, can we not discern some main, ethically relevant features or aspects of any suffering or death which must always govern moral considerations? Can a person ever act directly against a suffering person's life by hastening death purposely? The principal, morally relevant feature in all such cases seems the inherent value and dignity of every person's life, which always merits respect. The moral norm protecting this value seems unexceptionable: one can never intentionally kill an innocent person. A doctor, nurse, or concerned relative need not approach each concrete problem by constructing an entirely new moral outlook to handle the case. The moral norm based on man's being and inherited from mankind's lengthy historical pilgrimage most often finds direct application. The moral norm accurately describes the human significance of the contemplated action as a disvalue to be shunned. It violates the value of the human person.

Can we not apply the same reasoning to a number of other moral norms which protect human values and which rest on similar, ethically relevant features which occur in a variety of instances? When properly stated, the moral norms governing adultery, pre-marital relations, taking another's property against his reasonable will (theft), or payment of just wages, formulate man's grasp of value or disvalue in all possible instances. (See R. McCormick, "Human Significance and Christian Significance," in *Norm and Context in Christian Ethics,* ed. G. Outka-P. Ramsey, 233-61, for a full treatment of these notions, applied particularly to sexual ethics.) No matter what the unique, individual, or ineffable factors present in the concrete act of adultery, pre-marital intercourse, theft, or defrauding of wages, a major, ethically relevant feature becomes discernible in every act of adultery and the other actions which cannot be ignored. For instance, adultery may take on infinite varieties of circumstances, but the main feature of entering into sexual relations with a person other than one's spouse serves as a main factor in judging the morality of the action. The inner sense of sexual relations as a total donation of oneself in the service of life within a permanent community of persons always remains pertinent and constitutes a human value.

NATURAL LAW AND LIFE IN CHRIST

A paradoxical aspect of natural law is that the "natural order" has never existed as such. Man has never been pure nature, a simple creature living without grace. Through an act of gratuitous goodness, God called him to a destiny which surpasses the creature-Creator relationship, introducing him into the very life of the Trinity and permitting him to share in this life. Theology indicates this reality in saying man was created in a supernatural state which absolutely surpasses the tendencies and inner demands of man's nature. (See M. Donnelly, "The Supernatural Person," *Irish Theological Quarterly* 30 [1963] 340-47.) Why then attach importance to nature or to a corresponding natural law? Does not the Gospel morality rule out man's self-sufficiency in attaining salvation by his own endeavors? Does adherence to natural law imply a two-storyed theology of the natural and the supernatural in man and the universe? Some understanding of the relationship between nature and grace seems a prerequisite to any reply to these queries, for natural law has much the same relationship to Gospel morality.

The grace of Christ heals man's relationship with God according to the Father's original creative intention and frees fallen man from his sins. Redemption in Christ could well have entailed only this limited restoration of man's natural openness to God his Creator, but in fact it did not. Justification surpasses any mere restoration of the man-God relationship, elevating the new man in Christ to the unique dignity of God's adoptive son. A new creation occurs which enables redeemed men to love God with God's own love and to enter into a filial relationship with the Father through the grace of Christ given by the Spirit. Adoption as a son of God thus assumes a character of gratuitousness for man, because he could never have earned of his own powers this fuller sharing in God's own life. Theology has traditionally utilized the notion of "grace" to describe this self-gift of God which elevates man's capacities, giving him a positive orientation to the three divine Persons. (See J. Glaser, "Man's Existence: Supernatural Partnership," *Theological Studies* 30 [1969] 473-88.)

The theological notion of human nature corresponds to a profound reality, indispensable for safeguarding the gratuity of grace as God's gift. The gratuitousness of grace presupposes some condition of reference from which it takes the meaning "undue." How can one conceive grace as "undue" or gratuitous, in other words, unless it stands in relation to another reality which connotes "due" to man? To speak about a new relationship to God conferred through the grace of Christ presumes another possible relationship flowing from man's so-called "natural" powers, his very being-a-man. As K. Rahner states: "Precisely so that revelation might be grace, it is necessary at least in principle that man should have something to do with God from a locus which is not already grace" (K. Rahner, "Current Problems in Christology," in *Theological Investigations,* Vol. I, 183). Man's adoption by the triune God does not eradicate this fundamental relationship to God, termed by some man's natural desire for the beatific vision. The continuing self-gift of God in grace supposes always a structure in man capable of being elevated and perfected. We call this underlying, continuing reality "human nature," not in the exact sense understood previously when referring to the philosophical notion of this term, but in a more precise theological sense. "In theology, 'human nature' is a negative concept. It is that which is left in man as we know him once the supernatural is taken away. In other words, for the theologian 'nature' means 'man minus the supernatural,' what is left of him when his supernatural makeup is thought of as lacking. The theologian finishes, then, with a concept of nature which cannot be defined with philosophical precision. We experience nature as it is, but we have no way of determining what it would be if the order of grace had never existed" (D. Gelpi, *Life and Light*, [N.Y.: Sheed & Ward, 1966] 52-53; see also K. Rahner, in "Nature and Grace," *Theological Investigations*, Vol. II, 165-88, esp. 182f. for his description of "nature").

Traditional theology expresses these notions in such statements as "grace does not destroy nature, but elevates and perfects it." Man's nature never exists apart from grace, but it does really exist as an integrated reality in the total picture of man living in the grace of Christ. "Pure nature," conceived of as completely free from an order of grace, does not and never has existed as such. However, "human nature," the created structure of man's being which founds his openness to God, does fully exist and retains relevance for Christian morality. Man's basic structures which pertain to his being-a-man remain present in the new creation in Christ. Otherwise, we could not speak of man himself remaining in existence in this new economy of grace. We experience and live a "graced human nature."

A theological understanding of natural law asserts that these basic structures of man have a continuing claim on man in his free moral decisions. His choices cannot bypass any element of his full humanity, cleansed, perfected and elevated through the grace of Christ. Christ himself assumed these basic structures of being-a-man in the incarnation. The Word does not destroy the man Jesus; similarly, grace does not destroy, it rather presumes, human nature. Man finds true humanness in Christ, but in quest of this, his God-given destiny, he cannot neglect any dimension of his being. Reflection on the implications of his created nature will, therefore, provide a source of fertile moral discernment for the Christian. This source of moral knowledge will never stand in opposition to the revealed Gospel morality; God's creative will cannot contradict his redemptive will. The new life in Christ takes seriously the manhood, the being-a-man, which every Christian person is in his very self. This full and undivided image of God in man enters every moral choice as a basis for discerning God's concrete call. God approaches man, he calls him, through his complete being. Man's so-called "natural being," therefore, enters every moral situation as a pertinent element. Since man's being is God's work, man in his being speaks God's Word. "Be what you are" retains relevance in the Christian life. St. Paul's moral doctrine fits into this same general perspective, for he consistently views the life in Christ as a living out of the moral imperative based on the indicative of the new created being in Christ. Time and again he returns to the theme of exhorting Christians to realize the full moral implications of their graced humanity, which has entered into the death and resurrection of the Lord.

The fundamental claim of natural law in this theological context is that every man retains an endowment whereby he can discern through his reason many basic requirements needed for the fulfillment of his being. In the really existing order, this "reason" never is purely natural, as though grace and faith did not enter into the task of moral discernment. Every human choice occurs in a grace-faith dimension, for the God of salvation confronts believer, atheist and agnostic alike at every moment with the grace of Christ. The reason which forms the basis of natural law is, then, reason assisted by grace. This graced reason, natural law states, serves man in discerning God's concrete calls through reflection on the implications of man's humanity. In this sense, the natural law is not really natural; it enters completely into the supernatural economy of salvation which takes place through the grace of Christ. Josef Fuchs rightly says that "Christ has redeemed the natural law" (J. Fuchs, "The Law of Christ," in *Moral Theology Renewed,* ed. E. McDonagh, 70-84, at 82). The accurate significance of the word "natural" in the term "natural law," therefore, reduces to a knowledge which is not consciously based on revelation in Sacred Scripture. The grace of Christ, not man's personal efforts at observing a so-called natural morality, contributes the ultimate efficacy to natural law as an element in the attainment of salvation. Natural law does not exist apart from the grace of Christ. Salvation does not occur separately from the grace of Christ. The doctrine of natural law, nevertheless, holds that the proper response of man in faith to the grace of God can never reject the basic demands of his being-a-man. Only one Christian morality exists, not a natural and a supernatural or Christian morality, but it includes natural law. (See F. Böckle, *Fundamental Concepts of Moral Theology,* 51-55.)

This point of view has serious implications for the debate described in the previous chapter about the relation between Christian charity and moral norms. Can love overturn the conclusions of natural law? May the grace of Christ call man to actions contrary to natural law? Natural law claims to rest its case on the continuing demands of man's being in the Christian life. The call to love God or the neighbor cannot contradict the full humanity of the human person. "The claim of others on my love is inseparable from my being and their being. All that the authentic natural law tradition asserts is that a person's loving and lovability may not be defined short of his full humanity" (R. McCormick, in *Norm and Context in Christian Ethics,* ed. G. Outka-P. Ramsey, 240). Charity truly intends that in our actions we should take into account other men and their needs. The full being of men cannot be ignored by appealing directly to charity. The will of God to love the neighbor finds expression in every attempt to discern the ethical implications of the neighbor's graced humanity. The call of love respects the call of man's being. A direct appeal to the freedom of the children of God, to the inner promptings of the Holy Spirit, to Christian charity calling one to do "the loving thing" in violation of moral norms sufficiently founded on man's being, seems unsupportable. It ultimately contends, it would seem, that two contradictory wills of God have a bearing on the moral situation.

Natural law conclusions nevertheless form most often a minimum, negatively formulated boundary for the action of love. A Christian cannot rest content with the mere observance of universal, absolute moral norms. Karl Rahner's effort at a formal existential ethics (a Christian situation ethics), which complements the general-universal ethics of natural law, represents an attempt to formulate technically the dynamism of the Christian life. General and universal norms retain their validity as setting the outer limits inherent in God's concrete call. While adhering to these moral norms, the believing Christian will seek in faith and love to go beyond a minimalistic response to God's invitations. The divine call has an open-endedness which cannot be set down in general moral formulas, which merely serve as a minimum check and guideline. Radical obedience to the guiding grace of the Holy Spirit will lead the responsive Christian along uncharted paths of personal friendship with God and the neighbor. (See K. Rahner, *The Dynamic Element in the Church; Nature and Grace;* "On the Question of a Formal Existential Ethics," in *Theological Investigations,* Vol. II, 217-34.)

THE TESTIMONY OF THE BIBLE

Does this description of natural law accord with the biblical data? This basic question has ecumenical relevance, in addition to its inherent theological importance, for many Protestant theologians have denied traditional understandings of natural law. The limits of our inquiry should be clearly established from the outset. Sacred Scripture surely does not propose an explicit and systematized treatment of natural law, nor does it even employ the term "natural law." But does the core notion of natural law find a basis in the Bible? Does Sacred Scripture propose man's fundamental ability to grasp through his reason the unwritten law of his being? Does the New Testament morality of love leave room for this aspect of moral discernment?

Some authors see natural law principles in the *Old Testament* and conclude that the doctrine finds support there. For instance, the parallelism in form and content which exists between the law of Moses and the Code of Hammurabi, in force long before the Mosaic law, is cited as an example of natural law. More than one theologian has also indicated the relationship between nearly the entire Decalogue and natural law conclusions. This line of argumentation, however, ultimately proves inconclusive. Unlike their Near Eastern neighbors, the Israelites viewed all their laws as the revealed will of God and they made no distinction between religious and secular laws. In reality, their laws often simply mirrored their environment and articulated their customs of ordinary life which in their thoroughly theistic view of the world took on a divine-religious connotation. Their viewpoint, therefore, does not fit the thought-pattern of natural law, whereby man is seen as reflecting on the implications of his being-a-man and arrives at a universal morality. God's will binds man totally, but traditional tribal customs and laws reveal this will, not man's reason as such. One could, moreover, demonstrate readily a great dissimilarity between certain Old Testament practices and natural law as proposed today, for example, in regard to lying, attitudes toward non-tribal members, monogamous marriage, and concubinage. These examples show how tenuous is the claim that natural law doctrine is formally proposed in the Old Testament.

The *New Testament* proposes a personalistic morality of life in Christ manifested primarily through love of the neighbor. The love preached by Jesus takes account of the full humanity of each person, however, and implies that Christian love cannot be divine unless it be perfectly human. Jesus expects his listeners to be men in the fullest sense and to use their native capacities to the utmost. Human reasoning retains a vital role for his disciples. Jesus presupposes in his preaching that his listeners have a basic ability to distinguish between good and evil. His words frequently recall the Mosaic Law and the entire religious tradition of Israel. Nevertheless, his judgment about the harshness of the Sabbath law (Mark 3:3) and his discussion of ceremonial impurity (Mark 7:20-23) imply that his Jewish audience has the native ability to justify contravention of the Law when it proves unreasonable. This implicitly acknowledges man's continuing ability to reason to the rightness and wrongness of concrete actions by appealing to a higher norm discerned by man's intelligence. A source of moral knowledge other than revelation itself seems available to Jesus' listeners.

Bruno Schüller approaches this question in a less exegetical way. Taking the new economy of salvation as whole, Jesus surely does not primarily announce a natural moral law already accessible to man. Jesus instead proposes a new law of grace, which represents a radically new creation and a more enriching life. By this very fact of proclaiming a new ethical message, however, Jesus' preaching presupposes man's grasp of himself as an ethical being capable of hearing the Word addressed to him. The coming of Christ cannot have abolished the human values consonant with man's being, but must instead have ennobled and transformed them. How else could the disciple of Christ understand the meaning of revealed Christian love, humility, and trust in revelation, unless his own ethical experience based on his created being equips him with the basic language and ontological foundation to make these new, specifically revealed notions clear to him? Man can hear and give intelligent assent to Jesus' message because logically prior to this new message he grasps and expresses himself as an ethical being. The proclamation of the new ethical message of Jesus supposes the continuing validity of the ethical message written into man's very being-a-man. (See B. Schüller, "Can Moral Theology Ignore Natural Law?" *Theology Digest* 15 [1967] 94-99; R. McCormick comments favorably on Schüller's article in "Notes on Moral Theology," *Theological Studies* 27 [1967] 760-61, and in *Norm and Context in Christian Ethics,* ed. G. Outka-P. Ramsey, 237-38.)

Frequent reference is made to the writings of St. Paul in support of natural law, especially the so-called *loci classici,* the texts of Romans 1:19-21 and 2:15. St. Paul refers in these passages to the pagans' rejection of God and their gross immorality, which will be punished. He does not primarily concern himself, however, with either the knowledge of God or ethical demands. The whole section of Romans 1:18—3:20 rather serves to show that "all have sinned and need the glory of God" (3:23). The pagans have a knowledge of God from creation (1:20), but "although they knew God, they did not glorify him as God or give thanks" (1:21). They fail to fulfill their basic religious obligations and "they are without excuse" (1:21). This fundamental failure created a disharmony in the pagans' behavior, leading to many vices (1:24-32). St. Paul's presumption throughout these statements is that the pagans have sufficient moral knowledge to seek out morally good actions, even though they lack the Mosaic Law and Christ's revelation. He does not intend to shame the sinful Jews by odious comparisons with noble pagans, but rather to destroy the Jews' pride in the Law as sufficient for salvation and their boasting about the revelation of the Law without actual fulfillment of its commandments. Neither Jew nor pagan can withstand the final judgment of God without faith in Christ, which alone brings the grace of salvation.

St. Paul thus claims that the discernment of morally good or bad choices is as possible for a pagan as for a Jew or a follower of Christ. Every man possesses the native capacity to make moral judgments by reflecting on reality through the light of reason. Even the pagan can and must perform the works of the Law, though he possesses neither the written Mosaic Law nor Christ's message, for he has the law written in his heart and discernible by conscience (2:14-15). If pagans are likewise sinners who cannot withstand God's verdict, this fact supports Paul's doctrine of justification: that there exists only one way of salvation, redemption by the blood of Jesus. Recognition of the good and occasional fine action is not enough to bring anyone to salvation. In point of fact, man's natural ability to discern the unwritten law in his heart is just as weak (8:3), just as unable to give life (Gal. 3:21), as the Mosaic Law. Man's moral endowment assumes its real worth only when he lives in Christ, opening himself to the guidance of the Holy Spirit.

In an unsystematic way and in support of his general theme of redemption through the grace of Christ alone, St. Paul thus asserts the existence of a "law written in their hearts," which can be known even by pagans through "their conscience." When assumed by the grace of Christ, this inner law can serve in man's salvation. All men thereby possess an awareness of good and evil through a source other than God's explicit revelation. Certainly St. Paul does not present a Thomistic analysis of natural law nor the nuanced versions of contemporary thinkers. He does, however, assign a perduring role to man's own innate powers to discern the rightness or wrongness of his moral choices. Is this not the heart of natural law? Reason assisted by grace plays a vital part in man's moral life in Christ. It does seem tenable to state, therefore, that the core notion of natural law does find a basis in the Bible. (See R. Schnackenburg, *The Moral Teaching of the New Testament,* 289-93, for a fuller and more technical explanation of this position.)

THE TEACHING OF THE CHURCH

A striking contrast confronts one who studies the Church's statements on natural law. In comparison with recent times, the teaching office spoke rather infrequently about natural law in past ages. Authoritative documents rarely mention it even in passing. Though St. Thomas greatly clarified the doctrine, moveover, later official texts did not rely on his systematic interpretation. In the 15th and 17th centuries, it is true, several papal documents allude to natural law as the standard for condemning vices such as fornication, masturbation, and extra-marital sexual abuses. These sources utilize the term "natural law," but without clarifying its meaning or giving a theoretical, coherent explanation of the doctrine. Pope Pius IX initiated the modern tendency of referring to natural law perspectives in connection with communism, contraceptive marital relations, clerical immunity from military service, the origins of the binding force of civil laws, the indissolubility of marriage, and the possibility of salvation for an unbeliever in good faith. Following the revival of Thomism during the pontificate of Pope Leo XIII, modern popes have continued this dependence on natural law. References to natural law enter so often into the statements of Pope Pius XII, in particular, that he covers nearly every facet of the doctrine and presents an underlying systematic theory of natural law. Appealing to natural law as a firm moral basis, the popes have made pronouncements on the moral aspects of political structures, the social order, race relations, the conduct of war, conjugal morality, the extra-marital use of human sexuality, medico-moral problems, and the education of youth. Especially in the social teachings of the modern popes does one encounter a heavy reliance on natural law, presumably because a direct appeal to reason and to the main implications of man's dignity would carry more weight with contemporary man than would argumentation based on revelation and faith.

Despite this abundant material which stresses natural law, no single Church pronouncement contains a thoroughly explained and generally accepted development of the philosophico-theological doctrine. The birth control controversy has demonstrated the lack of agreement in the believing Church on the meaning and application of the natural law, and also the inability of the official papal teaching office to convince large numbers of Catholics concerning a major teaching based on one understanding of natural law, as applied to a specific moral question. (The natural law proposed in the liberal documents of the Papal Commission on Birth Control contrasts considerably with that proposed in *Humanae Vitae;* see *The Birth Control Debate,* ed. R. Hoyt [Kansas City: National Catholic Reporter, 1968].) The fact is that the Church presents many moral conclusions which claim a natural law foundation, but the teaching office of the Church has not fully elaborated an official systematic theory. As a rule, the magisterium has referred more frequently to and laid greater stress on specific moral teachings founded on natural law, than on the scientific explanation of the underlying ethical principles from which these conclusions derive. Condemnations of therapeutic abortion, euthanasia, artificial insemination, and indiscriminate acts of war directed against entire cities together with their civilian populations fall into this category. Some teachings on the theoretical bases of natural law also have received repeated emphasis: for example, on the objectivity, substantial immutability, universality, and knowability of natural law. The teaching office has, without doubt, clearly proposed at various times the continuing existence within the Christian revealed law of love of divinely willed, universal, substantially unchangeable moral norms of human behavior knowable to man by reason independently of God's revelation. (See G. Regan, *Catholic Lawyer* 13 [1967] 21-41, esp. 31f.)

Various papal statements have expressed the Church's competence to teach authoritatively natural law, both in principles and in concrete applications, but the exact binding force of these statements remains severely controverted. The *Dogmatic Constitution on the Church* states: "This infallibility with which the divine redeemer wills his Church to be endowed in defining a doctrine of faith and morals extends as far as extends the deposit of divine revelation" (n. 25). Does natural law fall within revelation, at least implicitly? Or is natural law outside God's self-communication within the Church? Does the Church therefore have the competence to assert infallibly natural law principles or applications? Theologians split on this issue today. Gregory Baum seems the most frequently cited proponent of the view which excludes the Church's power to make infallible statements about natural law. (See G. Baum, "Doctrinal Renewal," *Journal of Ecumenical Studies* 2 [1965] 365-81; "Teaching Authority of Vatican II," *The Ecumenist* 3 [1965] 89-93; "The Christian Adventure: Risk and Renewal," *The Critic* 23 [1965] 40-53; "The Magisterium in a Changing Church," *Concilium* 21 [1967] 34-42; cf. also K. Kelly, "The Authority of the Church's Moral Teaching," *Clergy Review* 52 [1967] 682-94.) Josef Fuchs, Richard McCormick and John Reed have written in defense of the broader understanding of the Church's competence in this area, claiming that natural law morality is an integral part of the law of Christ and therefore stands within the revealed Christian way of life. McCormick says: "Even if . . . the natural law was not integral to the Gospel, the Church's prerogative to propose infallibly the Gospel morality would be no more than nugatory without the power to teach the natural law infallibly. One could hardly propose what concerns *Christian men* without proposing what concerns *men*. . . . To propose the natural law is essential to the protection and proposal of Christian morality itself, much as certain philosophical truths are capable of definition because without them revealed truths are endangered" (R. McCormick, "Notes on Moral Theology," *Theological Studies* 26 [1965] 615; cf. also J. Fuchs, *Natural Law. A Theological Investigation,* 6; *id., Theologia moralis generalis,* pars prima, 70; J. Reed, "Natural Law, Theology, and the Church," *Theological Studies* 26

[1965] 40-64; for a summary of their views, see D. Leigh, "The Church as a Moral Guide," *American Ecclesiastical Review* [1968] 385-98, esp. 394 f.).

To the present author, it seems tenable that the Church has the competence to pronounce with doctrinal certitude about the existence of natural law, its basic knowability in its essential outlines, and whether specific natural law theses are reconcilable with revelation. I would agree with McCormick that "the infallible competence of the Church does not imply the power to proceed infallibly through the multiple judgments and informational processes required to apply these natural and Gospel values to highly concrete instances. This restriction does not solve the question about competence to define the natural law. It merely suggests that, regardless of what position one prefers on this point, he should distinguish between the natural law in its basic imperatives, and derivations or applications of this law. It also suggests that a more realistic and fruitful avenue of enquiry is the authentic non-infallible moral magisterium" (R. McCormick, "Notes on Moral Theology," *Theological Studies* 29 [1968] 709; see in the same issue the excellent article by J. Glaser, "Authority, Connatural Knowledge, and the Spontaneous Judgment of the Faithful," 742-51.)

All Catholic authors agree, it would seem, that the Church has authoritative (authentic), non-infallible teaching power in natural law matters. The proper response due this teaching office, however, continues to be an intense subject of Catholic theological disagreement, particularly in light of *Humanae Vitae*. Two main trends are discernible. One position, actually contained in the *Dogmatic Constitution on the Church,* n. 25, stresses obedience or "religious submission of mind and will" as the proper response of the believer to the authentic teachings of the popes and bishops. "It must be shown in such a way that his supreme magisterium is acknowledged with reverence, the judgments made by him are sincerely adhered to, according to his mind and will" (*ibid.*). Intellectual assent to and acceptance of the authentic teaching, then, are the ordinary obligatory responses of the faithful Catholic. In matters of public conduct, one must always act according to the opinion proposed; dissent becomes possible only in rare, extraordinary cases of private conduct. "It will not easily or commonly happen that the ordinary faithful, the ordinary priest, or even the ordinary theologian will be in a position to depart from the sort of authentic teaching at issue here" (J. Reed, *art. cit.;* see also J. Dedek, "Freedom of the Catholic Conscience," *Chicago Studies* 7 [1968] 115-25, who stresses obedience as the due response and then, working within this framework, explains the possibility of dissent, much as the freedom of the Christian conscience before Church law; R. McCormick treats the question in "Notes on Moral Theology," *Theological Studies* 29 [1968] 712-14).

A second, more recent position, especially in reaction to *Humanae Vitae,* claims that the proper response to a teacher, including the Church, is not obedience, assent, submission, or acceptance, but rather religious docility, openness, reverence, respect, and careful reflection, which generally leads to assent, but not always. (See McCormick, *art. cit.,* 717.) This view agrees that the teaching office of the Church is truly an authoritative teacher which deserves a presumption in favor of its teachings of faith and morals. The Holy Spirit's assistance guides the entire Church and, in a particular way, the magisterium. However, this assistance does not overcome all need for human insight, gradual acquisition of knowledge, and the real possibility of change or error. Statements such as the following receive stress: "The Church guards the heritage of God's Word and draws from it religious and moral principles, without always having at hand the solution to particular problems" (*Pastoral Constitution on the Church in the Modern World,* n. 33). According to this viewpoint, some past authentic teachings of the Church constitute working rules, but not unchanging moral laws. Specific moral rules enacted by the teaching office should be understood as sure guides for the periods for which they are enacted, but they require continuous re-examination and, at times, revision to preserve their purpose of spelling out the implications of the new life in Christ and to protect the human values they safeguard. Herbert McCabe writes within this approach, when he says:

The magisterium of the Church should not be quick as formerly to see in individual rules of behavior which either prevail in society or are laid down by itself, immutable principles of natural law valid for all times and places. It should be readier to see more of these as good guides for the time being, perhaps to be modified later. Indeed the magisterium would largely spare itself the trouble of trying to distinguish between rules which are immutable as they stand and those which are not, if in moral matters it tried to be more of a pastoral guide to men, pointing out to them, under the inspiration of the love of God in Christ, the best means of living that it now knows, instead of a legal authority laying down universal laws and sanctions for them .(H. McCabe, "New Thinking on Natural Law," *Herder Correspondence* 4 [1967] 347-52).

This second position envisions more readily than the obedience-centered approach the possibility of responsible dissent from official teachings of the papal or episcopal magisterium. Serious evidence evaluated by many honest and competent Christians may, by way of exception, found a contrary view. An obligation to follow one's personal conscience on the issue involved, rather than follow the official teaching, may obtain. In any case, respect, reverence, careful study, consultation, and a true communal reflection should characterize the Christian reaction to authentic teaching. A new grasp and fuller sharing in basic human and Christian values will be the outcome of this open and docile learning process. It need not involve a challenge to due ecclesiastical authority or disloyalty, charges too often made in the midst of the *Humanae Vitae* controversy. Richard McCormick nevertheless makes a valid point in regard to the general responsibility of theologians vis-à-vis the magisterium:

They would go a long way toward discharging their responsibilities if in the diffusion of theological thought they scrupulously adhered to the pedagogical guidelines stated by the episcopal synodal commission on doctrine: "First of all, let what is certain and fundamental be proposed as the unshaken basis of the faith and of Christian life; then what is new should be presented in such a way that a fitting explanation will manifest the continuity in the faith of the Church; finally, hypotheses should be put forth with that degree of probability which they in fact enjoy and with attention to the ways in which it is foreseen it will be understood" (R. McCormick, *art cit.*, 712; the quote from the Synod is found in *Furrow* 19 [1968] 111).

This broader interpretation of the authentic magisterium has become widely operative today. Particularly in the enormous literature on contraception and the pill, many Catholics call openly for a revision of past authentic papal teachings. This viewpoint would permit a much greater freedom of inquiry and expression of disagreement than traditionally proposed. I personally find this broader interpretation more acceptable from an ecclesiological understanding and from the actual reality of Church pronouncements on matters such as usury, the right to silence, and birth control. The former opinion does not seem to handle adequately the problems raised by such actual instances of authentic Church teaching. At any rate, the understanding of the existence of two opinions in this area will allow readers to gain insight into the sometimes heated controversies that currently exist and how theologians arrive at the positions they espouse which seem so diametrically opposed.

BIBLIOGRAPHY

Arntz, J., "Natural Law and Its History," *Concilium* 5 (1965) 39-57.

Aubert, J., *Loi de Dieu. Lois des hommes* (Tournai: Desclee, 1964).

Baum, G., "Protestants and Natural Law," *Commonweal* 73 (1961) 427-30.

———, *Law and Conscience* (N.Y.: Sheed and Ward, 1966).

Böckle, F., *Fundamental Concepts of Moral Theology* (Paramus, N.J.: Paulist Press, 1968).

Chirico, P., "Tension, Morality and Birth Control," *Theological Studies* 28 (1967) 258-85.

Crowe, M., "Natural Law Theory Today," in *The Future of Ethics and Moral Theology*, R. McCormick *et al.* (Chicago: Argus, 1968) 78-105.

Curran, C.: see his books, *Christian Morality Today, A New*

Look at Christian Morality, and *Absolutes in Moral Theology?* (ed.).

Daly, C., "Natural Law Morality Today," *American Ecclesiastical Review* 153 (1965) 361-98.

David, J., *Loi naturelle et authorité de l'Eglise* (Paris: Editions du Cerf, 1968).

Evans, I. (ed.), *Light on the Natural Law* (London: Burns and Oates, 1965).

Favara, F., *De iure naturali in doctrina Pii Papae XII* (Rome: Desclee, 1966).

Fuchs, J., *Human Values and Christian Morality* (Dublin: Gill and Macmillan, 1970).

——, *Natural Law. A Theological Investigation* (N.Y.: Sheed and Ward, 1965).

——, *Theologia moralis generalis, pars prima,* 3rd ed. (Rome: Gregorian University, 1965).

Gelpi, D., "Nature, Grace and the Hypostatic Union," in *Life and Light* (N.Y.: Sheed & Ward, 1966) 39-57.

Hamel, E., *Loi naturelle et loi du Christ* (Desclee de Brouwer, 1964).

Hurley, D., "In Defense of the Principle of Overriding Right," *Theological Studies* 29 (1968) 301-09.

Kelly, G., "Notes on Moral Theology," *Theological Studies* 24 (1963) 631-35.

Lindbeck, G., "Natural Law in the Thought of Paul Tillich," *Natural Law Forum* 7 (1962) 84-96.

McCormick, R., "Notes on Moral Theology," *Theological Studies* 26 (1965) 608-15; 28 (1967) 760-69; 29 (1968) 707-18; 30 (1969) 644-68.

——, "Human Significance and Christian Significance," in *Norm and Context in Christian Ethics,* ed. G. Outka-P. Ramsey (N.Y.: C. Scribner's, 1968) 7-18.

McKenzie, J., "Natural Law in the New Testament," *Biblical Research* 9 (1964) 1-11.

McNeill, J., "Natural Law in the Teaching of the Reformers," *Journal of Religion* (July, 1946).

Monden, L., *Sin, Liberty and Law* (N.Y.: Sheed and Ward, 1965).

Morton, C., "What Protestants Think about Natural Law," *Catholic World* 190 (1960) 294-300.

Murray, J., *We Hold These Truths* (N.Y.: Sheed and Ward, 1960).

Noonan, J., "Authority, Usury and Contraception," *Cross Currents* 16 (1966) 55-80.

Reed, J., "Natural Law, Theology, and the Church," *Theological Studies* 26 (1965) 40-64.

Regan, G., "Natural Law in the Church Today," *The Catholic Lawyer* 13 (1967) 21-41.

————, "The Need for Renewal in Natural Law," *The Catholic Lawyer* 12 (1966) 135-40.

Schnackenburg, R., *The Moral Teaching of the New Testament* (N.Y.: Herder & Herder, 1965) 289-93.

Schüller, B., "Can Moral Theology Ignore Natural Law?" *Theology Digest* 15 (1967) 94-99.

Walgrave, J., "Is Morality Static or Dynamic?" *Concilium* 1 (1965) 13-22.

Weber, L., *On Marriage, Sex and Virginity* (London: Burns & Oates, 1966) 17-33.

9. Christian Conscience

God calls each person to conform himself to Christ through the action of the Holy Spirit. If this call remains unknown, the Christian cannot respond freely to it. How then does a follower of Christ recognize God's invitations in concrete situations? For example, how does a person know that God desires the preservation of an aged man's life and forbids euthanasia? The standard answer is familiar: the voice of God is heard in our conscience, the act by which an individual judges about the morality of a proposed act. Though this popular notion of conscience may seem superficially acceptable, however, agreement about its actual functioning is lacking. The clash between an appeal to personal conscience and the claim of public interest seems, in fact, to be on the increase in modern times. Witness the issues raised about selective conscientious objection to modern warfare, dissent from *Humanae Vitae,* and civil disobedience in support of civil rights. A supposed opposition is thus proposed between the individual's conscience and the community's formation of objective claims.

A theological treatment of conscience cannot ignore these pertinent contemporary themes. They afford a perspective for judging the relevancy of theological insights into conscience. Because of these present controversies, moreover, it seems more proper to take our starting point from the daily experience of conscience. An overview of the biblical theology on conscience will then lead to theological reflections on more modern problems relating to man's moral knowledge.

THE EXPERIENCE OF CONSCIENCE

Feelings of guilt, remorse, well-being or fulfillment often accompany a person's activities. Anxiety, fear, a sense of obligation,

145

an awareness of the ethical dimension of past, present, or proposed conduct: all these enter as part and parcel of ordinary human experience. Christian reflection on the new life offered in the Son must face the enormous task of sorting through this immense interplay of affective, intellectual, and religious factors which combine into the adult Christian conscience. Moral adulthood in Christ, not an infantile domination by the bundle of influences which converge in the superego, forms the goal of a fully grown moral awareness. Dread, scrupulosity, or moral insensitivity has no place in the man freed by Christ.

The three levels of ethical conduct analyzed by Louis Monden will permit insight into a more accurate understanding of Christian conscience. Monden discusses in turn the instinctive, moral, and Christian-religious levels of conduct (*Sin, Liberty and Law,* chapter 1).

1. The twinge of a guilty conscience which men sometimes experience from supposedly sinful conduct actually stems at times from a pre-human level of instinct. Similar in nature to a reflexive behavior of non-rational animals which fail to attain their goals, this instinctive ethics rests on the outer pressures of society's taboos felt as alien to the inner resources of the person. A blind feeling of material transgressions produces an ambivalent reaction of emotional guilt, often influenced by rationalized motives. This sort of guilt, sin, contrition, or conscience does not have its basis in a personal and free decision, but rather it constitutes an instinctive anxiety reflex. The merely material transgression of some taboo calls forth this fear of sanctions, and a sense of irresistible occult powers comes into play. The scrupulous person lives constantly under the sway of such emotional compulsion. Who has not experienced in himself at times this instinctive level of moral conduct? Guilt or a feeling of sinfulness may even accompany actions which in cool reasonableness we know to be perfectly upright. Unrest about missing Sunday Mass despite a substantial excusing cause (e.g., to care for a sick child), or anxious reactions about past adolescent sexual behavior (e.g., masturbation) *now* known to be wrong are examples of such guilt feelings on the level of instinct which occur in the lives of emotionally well-adjusted people. If Christian conscience were identified with this

level of ethical conduct, man would justifiably live in apprehension about his destiny.

2. Man attains his free and conscious self-realization on the moral level of his existence. This authenically human manner of ethical conduct occurs mainly by the development of one's personality in an adult, loving self-giving to other people. Ethical conduct on this level finds its norms in the degree of human self-realization expressed in this self-giving. Man experiences himself as a free and autonomous individual in a process of continual growth and self-development from within. The impersonal, magiclike feelings of the instinctive level become integrated within the person's conscious self-fulfillment. The possibility of growth through free choices occupies the center of moral awareness. On this level, conscience is a power of discrimination in choosing between what will promote or hinder man's self-realization. Guilt or a sense of sinfulness will be felt as unfaithfulness to one's authentic self-fulfillment. The taboo morality of moral childhood cedes on this level to a mature moral consciousness based on free and reasonable conduct. Healthy development to moral adulthood consists in a gradual and harmonious personalization of instinctive reactions. Ideally, the instinctive feelings of duty, guilt, or sinfulness arising from one's unconscious past should harmonize with the consciously recognized duty, sin, or guilt. Inadequate growth may stifle this harmonization in the practical order for many people, but it remains the psychological and moral-religious ideal. The tyranny of moral taboos associated with childhood and with regressive states requires constant resistance. Fixation in infantile reactions impedes an adult moral life in Christ.

3. The properly Christian-religious dimension of ethical conduct integrates and elevates the instinctive and moral levels of existence into a partnership of love with God. A total loving encounter between God calling and man responding becomes the ultimate ethical criterion for the Christian in dialogue with the three divine Persons. Law, obligation, guilt, sinfulness, contrition and sanction take on a personalist meaning and enter human consciousness as aspects of man's yes or no to his divine partner. The authentic self-realization proper to the moral level of ethical conduct finds at this new divinized level a fullness and comple-

tion in the service of man's loving response. "Conscience on this level will be love itself as a power of discriminating what can promote from what will hinder its growth. It is no longer a natural or rational insight—although moral insight continues to act in the religious conscience—but an affinity with the beloved, a communion in feeling and in thinking, a 'connaturality' with him" (Monden, 9).

CONSCIENCE IN SACRED SCRIPTURE

There is no single Hebrew word which expresses the idea of conscience, and the Greek word for conscience appears only twice in the Old Testament (*syneidesis*, Wisdom 17:11). The reality of conscience is, however, frequently referred to, especially under the terms heart, reins, wisdom, spirit, and prudence (P. Delhaye, *The Christian Conscience* [N.Y.: Desclée, 1968] 51-66). The phenomenon of conscience condemns man for his sins from the very beginning of salvation history, as seen in the passages about Adam (Gen. 3:7-10), Cain (Gen. 4:13), and David (2 Sam. 24:10). In other passages, on the other hand, conscience praises man for his justice (Psalm 26:1-7; Job 27:6). Conscience appears as the presence of the responsible man before God and as the divine law interiorized. It is always related to hearing God's Word, the acceptance of his will, consciousness of one's own created position before God, and the divine judgment. For the most part, however, little mention is made in the Old Testament about interior motivations, dispositions or a sense of remorse.

The word for conscience is absent from the Gospels. Jesus nevertheless describes the reality of man's inward moral attitude under various figures of speech. He recommends prudence (Luke 16:8; 14:28-32) and he compares it with the eye as the light by which the whole body is enlightened. He warns us not to neglect the care of this light; otherwise, we shall become darkness (Matt. 6:22). The same warning occurs in Luke 11:33, where Jesus speaks of putting a lamp on the lampstand. According to rabbinical usage, a light which is interior to man signifies the possibility of a spiritual-moral judgment. Jesus also uses the term "heart" to refer to man's spiritual faculty of moral discernment: "It is from within, from men's hearts, that evil intentions emerge" (Mark 7:21). In the heart, man makes his choices and decisions: "If a man looks at a woman lustfully, he has already committed adultery with her in his heart" (Matt. 5:28). Man's entire life springs from the basic choices made in his inner self, in his heart: "Where your treasure is, there also will your heart be" (Matt. 6:21). All these passages at least refer to some interior state of the human person.

St. Paul uses the Greek term for conscience (*syneidesis*) over twenty times in his letters. "Most often conscience is characterized as a 'witness'; it accompanies our actions as an incorruptible witness within us, and can also be called upon to attest the truth of our assertions" (R. Schnackenburg, *The Moral Teaching of the New Testament,* 289).

The key passage of St. Paul in regard to conscience is Romans 2:14-15:

Pagans who never heard of the Law, but are led by reason to do what the Law commands, may not actually "possess" the Law, but they can be said to "be" the Law. They can point to the substance of the Law engraved on their hearts—they can call a witness, that is, their own conscience—they have accusation and defense, that is, their own inner mental dialogue.

According to St. Paul, man experiences himself in conscience as bound to an interior norm which is not the Jewish Law and is independent of himself. He views himself as bound to the demands and judgments of a personal God. The apostle thus differs from the pantheistic teaching of the contemporary philosophers of his day. He also teaches that all men, pagan, Christian, and Jew alike, have such a capacity of making moral judgments. Finally, in the passage quoted, the apostle refers to conscience both as a guide which forewarns man of moral values in proposed actions and as a source of accusation or approbation of past deeds.

The New Testament considers conscience as a personal reality, proper to each individual, so that it merits different qualifiers: good, bad, weak and strong consciences are mentioned. A *good* (pure, clear) conscience implies the absence of faults through the aid of faith: "We are sure that our conscience is clear and we are certainly determined to behave honorably in everything we do" (Heb. 13:18). A good conscience thus makes one free and independent of the judgments of others. The Lord alone will judge (Acts 23:1). A *bad* conscience implies a perversion of man's spirit and is the stigma of a sinful life: "To all who are pure themselves, everything is pure; but to those who have been corrupted and lack faith, nothing can be pure—the corruption is both in their minds and in their consciences. . . . They are outrageously rebellious and quite incapable of doing good" (Titus 1:15-16). Conscience may also be *weak,* that is, it can err. St. Paul describes as weak the conscience of those who wrongly distinguish between foods to be eaten and foods not to be eaten (1 Cor. 8:10; Rom. 14). Even such a mistaken conscience remains a valid norm for action (1 Cor. 8:7) and obedience to an erroneous conscience can still lead to salvation (1 Cor. 8:11). One should, therefore, regard the conscience of others with respect (1 Cor. 10:18, 29). These texts support St. Paul's clear insight that one's personal conscience, whether correct or mistaken, is decisive for determining the moral quality of an act before God.

> The Pauline conscience then is susceptible to weakness; it can be corrupted, edified or influenced in evil, compelled by bad example. It is therefore not only the witness and interior judge, or the impersonal expression of duty. St. Paul goes further and gives the word *syneidesis* a personal sense, that of the will or the moral personality, the center of the soul where choices are worked out and responsibilities taken on (P. Delhaye, *The Christian Conscience,* 42).

Among Christians, conscience is not merely a natural judgment, but receives enlightenment from faith. St. Paul sometimes uses conscience and faith indiscriminately, so that the judgment about food to be eaten is made "by conscience" in 1 Cor. 8:10 and "by faith" in Rom. 14:23. For the author of the Pastoral

Epistles, faith and conscience have nearly the same meaning (1 Tim. 1:5, 19; 3:9; 4:2; 2 Tim. 1:5; Titus 1:15). By rejecting a good conscience and Christian standards of moral good and evil, some have made a shipwreck of their faith (1 Tim. 1:19). "To St. Paul, faith is the whole attitude of the Christian, assimilating his judgments of moral worth too. The Christian is not divided within himself, with a natural economy and a supernatural one; there is only one judgment of conscience and it is determined by his belief" (Schnackenburg, 294). Hence, in conjunction with faith, attention must be given to the operation of the Holy Spirit, whose inner guidance works and bears witness in our conscience (Rom. 8:22).

THEOLOGICAL REFLECTIONS

History of the Doctrine

The Church Fathers did not utilize fully the richness of this scriptural teaching on conscience. Numerous statements and opinions on conscience are found in Tertullian, Origen, Chrysostom, and Augustine. The latter describes especially the religious functions of conscience in some detail, but he and other patristic writers did not succeed in elaborating a satisfactory theology of conscience.

Medieval authors such as Bernard of Clairvaux, Petrus Cellensis, and Gerson developed further the religious teaching on conscience, stressing sensitivity and fidelity to God's calls in the depths of one's inner self. At the same time, a systematic teaching on conscience gradually developed among the Scholastics. This doctrine rested on a controverted text of St. Jerome's *Commentary on Ezekiel,* chapter 6, which distinguished between the terms *synteresis* (*synderesis*) and *conscientia.* Man's moral perception was considered to have *synteresis* as its natural nucleus, which remained intact even after the fall of man. This habitual awareness of moral values constitutes the *a priori* intellectual and volitional basis of all moral perception.

The Franciscan tradition, notably St. Bonaventure, attributed the affective processes in conscience to *synteresis,* and the more intellectual functions, both habitual and actual, to *conscientia*. "The Seraphic Doctor taught that *synderesis* is not the habit of first principles, but rather a habit of the will, inclining it to good. For Bonaventure, conscience perfects the intellect by directing it in its operation; conscience is a motivating force since it dictates and inclines to good. Gilson expresses the Franciscan notion of conscience as that which confers its ultimate determination not upon the knowing faculty as such but insofar as it is in some way united to the faculties of will and operation" (X. Colavechio, "Conscience: A Personalist Perspective," *Continuum* 5 [1967] 203-10, at 203-04).

Following St. Thomas Aquinas, the Thomistic or Dominican tradition calls *synteresis* the permanent natural habit of the primary moral principles, and *conscientia* the actual moral judgment arrived at by way of conclusion. A quasi-syllogism occurs in moral perception: from the major premise of *synteresis* and the minor premise of reason, one concludes to a concrete judgment of conscience. The process of moral insight is thus viewed as intellectual in nature. When the object of the first, irreducible principles of the natural law is presented to the intellect, it intuitively (connaturally) grasps them and infallibly passes a correct moral judgment about them. In the most basic of these principles ("good is to be done and pursued"), man grasps his total dependence on God and his ordering to him. He understands also that the good-to-be-done is what his reasoning powers see in conformity with his being (nature). Man's will tends naturally to affirm and carry out this good affirmed by right reason. Since both moral knowledge and moral will have essential roles in *synteresis,* this habit is seen as a habit which pentrates the whole man in every fiber of his being. The reality of *synteresis* thus implies that man has the basic ability to know and to will those primary moral values which will benefit him in his vital relationships.

The Dominican or Thomistic tradition has greatly influenced the later course of moral theology and has entered into the standard approaches to the doctrine on conscience. In the pages to follow, therefore, we shall outline the main notions of this influential understanding of conscience and afterward introduce some more recent approaches to the doctrine. This methodology may permit a better insight into the entire question of conscience. (See J. Fuchs, *Theologia moralis generalis,* pars prima, 151-218, for a thorough presentation of this viewpoint; J. Dolan, "Conscience in the Catholic Theological Tradition," in *Conscience: Its Freedom and Limitations,* ed. W. Bier, 9-19. will also prove useful.)

Synderesis and Conscience

Conscience is related to *synderesis* as an act to its principle. How does this habit of first moral principles (*synderesis*) allow man to make concrete moral judgments? Moral knowledge for concrete action occurs in two ways: by subsumption or by application. Subsumption means that some physical reality (e.g., the life of this aged, sick person) is subsumed (brought under) a general moral principle (e.g., euthanasia is always forbidden). Application occurs simply by applying general moral principles to a physical reality. For example, the general moral principle "you shall not murder" (kill intentionally an innocent person) applies every time innocent human life is at stake. Knowing this universal moral principle connaturally or intuitively in the habit of *synderesis,* the person applies it to this particular moral choice, e.g., whether to abort this inviable fetus. This concrete judgment about the here-and-now moral choice occurs through conscience, the faculty whereby practical moral judgments are made. A person with a rightly formed conscience concludes that the minimum demand of love in his decision is not to kill the fetus. The virtue of Christian prudence will stimulate the sensitive and concerned follower of Christ to go beyond this minimum judgment about the lawfulness or unlawfulness of his proposed intervention against human life to pass a further judgment about how best to realize the positive call to love in his situation. The full promotion of human and Christian values will be his concern. (See J. Pieper, *The Four Cardinal Virtues* [N.Y.: Harcourt, Brace & World, 1965] 3-40, for a fine treatment of the virtue of prudence.)

This process of moral knowledge is not an analytic operation performed by discursive reasoning, as though all morality could be deduced from a few general principles. (This would be to fall into the pure rule-agapism described by Frankena.) Instead, moral knowledge is *synthetic,* that is, a person must examine the facticity of each new proposed choice which faces him and the rest of mankind. In the light of his newly acquired knowledge, gained from reality, the individual Christian and the Christian community must apply or reassess previously formulated moral principles. Most often the previous formulations of moral principles will simply find direct application once again. At times, however, a new formulation may be in order. Many would contend this has occurred in the matter of birth regulation. Selective conscientious objection and some social doctrines (e.g., *Populorum Progressio* on the matter of aid to underdeveloped countries) may be other instances of needed reformulations of moral principles in light of new insights.

Moral judgments are not always made with explicitness and with reflexive awareness. The judgment about concrete realities, in fact, more frequently happens before all conscious reflection and takes place through an immediate understanding, nearly intuitively. For instance, it takes little if any reflection for the ordinary person to conclude that it is wrong to take money from another person's pocket, or to kill another for the sheer thrill of it. These intuitive, non-reflexive moral judgments constitute the vast majority of the moral decisions we reach. Only when a rather entangled moral choice arises (e.g., whether to kill prisoners in wartime, whether to relieve a terminal cancer patient from intolerable suffering, whether to abort a fetus conceived through rape), do we ordinarily reflect deeply and at length about how we attain our moral decisions. These "limit cases" sometimes provide occasion for a more profound appreciation of the Christian values enshrined in moral principles and they may also point out the gray limits of the black-and-white moral principles.

Conscience as Concrete Moral Judgment

Conscience may be called a practical judgment about the moral value of a concrete act. It does not concern itself with abstract and generalized moral reasoning, which might better be termed moral science or moral knowledge (traditionally called *scientia moralis*). Conscience decides whether a particular choice is in accordance with man's personal response to God calling him here-and-now, or a departure from the effective working out of the Spirit's guidance. Though basically a judgment of man's reason enlightened by the gift of grace, it involves the total person. Conscience informs a person, for example, that feeding *this* poor person is good and even obligatory for *me;* in omitting this act of charity, *I* see myself as rejecting God's invitation. Conscience thus does not as such make judgments about what other people should do. The "for me" aspect of conscience demonstrates the profound personal character of moral choice.

A moral choice which results from the judgment of conscience presupposes the person's grasping himself and his proposed action in a human fashion. This means that to arrive at a decision of conscience always presumes understanding and freedom, man's properly human qualities. The individual must know the morality of the proposed action and he must will this morality as *he* sees it. A personalized knowing and willing thus enters into every conscience-judgment. John can only make his own that morality which *he*, John, has judged to be present in the contemplated act. Parental pressure, society's norms or standards, his professor's views can never replace in his decision-making that ultimate moment of moral choice which descends to the particular choice "for me." The concrete morality of any action which John proposes for himself depends, then, on *his* judgment of conscience, which informs *him* (not his parents, friends, or even society in general) that the act is good, better, wrong, obligatory, lawful, unlawful, and so forth. When he judges that "beating my wife" is wrongdoing, and he still performs the act, he acts wrongly; that is, he acts immorally and against conscience. To act morally, on the other hand, he must judge that, for example, "correcting my children" is here-and-now for their welfare and hence morally good, and then intentionally correct them.

The Twofold Judgment of Conscience

In conscience a person experiences in the depths of his personality the moral quality of each concrete decision as a personal obligation for himself, for he views it as significant for the ultimate fulfillment of himself. In weighing the morality of any proposed action, therefore, a person actually makes a twofold judgment. One concerns the inner moral value of what he proposes to do; the other concerns his own personal fulfillment to be realized through actually accomplishing or doing the proposed action. This analysis is sometimes described by differentiating between the objective and subjective, or the material and formal aspects of the conscience-judgment. These divisions refer always to the experience of conscience, which in the concrete occurs as a unified reality.

In the center of one's person, an experience is had of the immediate attraction of moral goodness or value, or else of repulsion in the presence of badness or disvalue. The richness and fullness in moral value encourage and draw one on to it. The threat and constriction of evil and its harmful consequences likewise repel one. The basis of this moral sense lies ultimately in the center of man's self, in the most personal sphere of his being as an individual, where his personal powers are first experienced before any division of them into intellect, will, or emotions. Man manifests at this most intimate level of his being a positive orientation toward God and his ultimate capability of free decision about his personal self. Taken in this most ultimate sense, then, conscience emerges as a primary disposition of man which precedes divisions into objective and subjective, material and formal, such as mentioned above. For the sake of theological clarity, however, it has seemed worthwhile to reflect separately on these two moments of the one experience of conscience.

1. *The Judgment about the Objective Morality.* In analyzing the concrete judgment of conscience, one can prescind from the internal emotional and affective states of the person (e.g., his motives, passions) and concentrate on the inner morality of the proposed action as it relates to the moral order willed by God. This aspect of conscience thus refers to man's judgment about the rightness or wrongness of a course of action the person is contemplating or has already performed, e.g., taking merchandise from a supermarket, using LSD, procuring an abortion, or committing atrocities in wartime. For the individual person who is

reaching a decision, this judgment answers the questions: "Is this act right or wrong in itself? Does God desire such actions?" In ordinary affairs, we often implicitly ask such questions in which we strive to ascertain the inner morality of past, present or proposed actions in themselves, prescinding from the intentions or emotional states of the individual. For instance, do we not inquire about the moral principles governing race relations or warfare and, at times, condemn as wrong racial bigots or military leaders, even while acknowledging their good intentions? We are really saying that *what* they do is "objectively" wrong even though the bigots or leaders are "subjectively" guiltless.

Taken according to their inner nature, the objective and subjective aspects of conscience should coincide. I should, in other words, find my personal fulfillment in what is morally good. Man has a connatural bent toward moral value and so we ordinarily have a moral sense which leads us to make the right judgment about our conduct. Our judgment about the morality of proposed activity can, however, be mistaken at times. Our Lord himself referred to this possibility when he declared that the Jews desire to persecute his disciples while believing they do good through this action: "The hour is coming when anyone who kills you will think he is doing a holy duty for God" (John 16:2). Examples of such errors could be indefinitely multiplied simply by drawing on our own experience. Have we not witnessed in our times a lack of moral sensitivity to major moral issues involving human harmony in such matters as war, race, poverty, and politics? Human deafness to God's call to sonship in the Son and brotherhood among all men shocks the reflective Christian. The personal failures of ourselves and others to heed God's calls through erroneous perception of moral values in our past lives also come to mind in this context.

Traditional moral theology tied in the technical explanation of these human experiences of erroneous perception with the general doctrine on natural law and its grasp by man. Though each person understands the primary, rather general moral principles of *synderesis,* the application of these primary values and principles to actual situations may sometimes involve such complex reasoning that the person fails to attain the correct moral decision. The search for the morally correct solution may even necessitate agonizing and painstaking labor, as in reaching decisions about bombing military targets located near population centers, or in assessing the duty to preserve human life through such measures as intravenous feeding or brain surgery. In all cases, the Christian can never abdicate his authentic freedom and responsibility before God in the name of abstract, inherited moral statements of right and wrong. He must weigh the various facets of each new life-situation and strive for the personal insight into the morally permissible solution. If he should err in his assessment of the situation and his consequent moral imperative, his conscience will nevertheless indicate before God that he has done what is humanly possible. He will perform the morally good as seized and presented by his personal insight, thus fulfilling the law of love preached by Jesus.

This raises the traditional question about the certainty required in our judgments of conscience before acting. The judgment about the morality of an action requires *moral* certainty. This sort of certainty excludes considerable fear of error on our part, though the mere possibility of error may still be present. We have this kind of certainty about many, if not most, realities in our everyday lives. The lack of absolute certainty about our health, the weather, the outbreak of war, and so forth, does not deter us from reaching practical decisions. The same holds true for our moral judgments. We must attain a moral certainty about the objective morality of proposed conduct and this prudent search in sincerity for moral value suffices in God's eyes. Both an overly scrupulous investigation of morality and a lax or negligent approach to our judgments are incompatible with the life in Christ to which we are invited. To require more or less than such certainty would be inhuman. An anxious or scrupulous concern goes beyond the bounds of man's limited capacities and does not mirror the confidence and hope that should characterize the Christian reborn in Christ. On the other hand, if a person lacks moral certainty, he cannot with sincerity intend moral value, for the proposed action may just as well be morally evil. In performing the action with insufficient inquiry into its morality, he would act blindly in regard to moral value, surely an immoral and inhuman stance.

St. Paul refers to these notions about erroneous judgments in his instruction to the Romans about the use of clean and unclean foods. He holds that the law which distinguished between various types of food which can be eaten and not eaten lacks all value before God. Nevertheless, the person who remains uncertain about the lawfulness of eating a kind of food and still eats it should be condemned (Rom. 14:14).

2. *The Judgment about Personal Fulfillment.* Every moral decision involves at least implicitly a practical judgment about the effect of the proposed action on one's personal existence. Through his individual moral choices, in other words, a person takes hold of himself as a free and autonomous being who disposes himself radically before God and other men. He implicitly realizes that he creates and fulfills himself through his free choices, or else hinders his self-realization, e.g., by his heroism in saving another's life, by pilfering at his factory, or by severe detraction against the good reputation of another person. This aspect of the one judgment of conscience regards the intentional order of the person's choice: "By this act of love manifested toward my children, I intend to fulfill myself as a Christian father who sees God's personal call coming to me through these persons." This personal or intentional aspect of conscience dictates with absoluteness that "I should always act in accord with the judgment which I have formed about the inner rightness of showing love to my children." To act against this judgment in full awareness would be to act immorally. As another example, if I have concluded that "to cheat on my expense account would be morally wrong because it defrauds my employer," then I simultaneously conclude that "I should find my personal fulfillment as a moral person and as a Christian by truthfully listing my actual expenses."

A person cannot err in making this personal judgment. In following it, he tries to answer God's call to embrace specific moral values as *he* hears the call. If he mistakenly judges about the objective or inner morality of the action, he may still *intend* to respond to his Father in Christ by doing what *he* discerns to be morally upright, even though objectively he may commit wrongdoing. Other men of his own generation may condemn his action, but he remains bound to embrace that moral value which he has sincerely judged to be present. May this not be the case today regarding some violent acts of protest made against social injustice or regarding revolutionary doctrines preached against the civil regimes in South America? Society has the right to protect itself against violence, but this does not rule out in advance the possibility of individuals' discerning the call of conscience through violent measures. The conflicts which arise between society and personal appeals to conscience do not eliminate recourse to conscience at all times in favor of society's views; nor does the converse hold true. We may disagree too with the judgments arrived at sincerely by previous generations of people. For centuries, many Christians justified slavery or the licit use of torture for the purpose of exacting confessions from supposed wrongdoers. Today we consider these Christians to have reached false conclusions about the implications of the new commandment preached by Christ. How is slavery or torture compatible with loving the slave or prisoner as my brother? we ask. At times, therefore, we roundly condemn the actions of other people, whether our predecessors or our contemporaries, even while acknowledging their inner sincerity, honesty, and intention to love their fellow men. In the realm of personal conscience, they may have believed that they were acting morally and fulfilling their personal existence by responding to God's calls. In this sense, they were in good conscience, for their will tended to embrace the moral values which their reasonable evaluations presented to them. They desired to seek the morally good; their human limitations prevented them from reaching a correct assessment. Their positive intention to serve God and their neighbor nevertheless excuses them from guilt for their invincibly erroneous insight into value.

The chief criterion for discerning the presence of such an upright intention is a personal love of God and one's neighbor, the constant sign of the presence and inner movement of the Holy Spirit. Living in charity ensures a greater sensibility and awareness of the impulses of the Spirit urging from within. "My prayer is that your love for each other may increase more and more and never stop improving your knowledge and deepening your perception so that you can always recognize what is best" (Phil. 1:9). A loving attitude spontaneously adapts itself to the truly authentic Christian values to which the Spirit invites us: "Love is always patient and kind; it is never jealous; love is never boastful or conceited; it is never rude or selfish; it does not take offense, and is not resentful. Love takes no pleasure in other people's sins but delights in truth; it is always ready to excuse, to trust, to hope, and to endure whatever comes" (1 Cor. 13:4-7). The sincere intention to love in one's actions, combined with repentance and a willingness to heed God's invitations, thus assures a person of an upright personal conscience. Excessive anxiety about unperceived moral failures would at the least diminish were Christians to appreciate thoroughly these basic notions about personal conscience. (See P. Delhaye, *The Christian Conscience,* 44-48, 245f.)

The foregoing explanation of the role of Christian love does not, however, imply that charity alone leads one to do "the loving thing" in all circumstances. What we stated previously about the possibility of moral norms in their relation to charity applies here. The Christian seeks always to do "the loving thing" in every situation, just as Joseph Fletcher has stated, but love does not provide a sufficiently determined guide for one's moral life in its details. The Christian must reflect on the specifications of charity elaborated in the human community and in God's Word as proposed by the Church, in order to grasp the full implications of Christian charity. The traditions and reflections of the human and ecclesiastical communities provide many insights in the form of articulated moral rules or norms. These rules spell out the meaning of Christian love in a variety of similar situations. The here-and-now decision of conscience to do "the loving thing" can, therefore, utilize these formulated rules with great profit. "We can be sure that we love God's children if we love God himself and do what he has commanded us; this is what loving God is—keeping his Commandments" (1 John 5:2-3). (See J. Madden, "The Law of Charity and the Role of Conscience," *Australasian Catholic Record* 42 [1965] 308-15.)

It should be clear from these words about the objective and

personal aspects of conscience that morality properly so-called rests in the latter element of the conscience-judgment. The moral person is one who *intends* to do the morally good; his erroneous judgment about *what* is good does not make him immoral. In ordinary usage, however, we frequently objectify morality and speak of the act as being immoral "in itself," that is, as it stands in relation to the objective moral order prescinding from the person's intentions and emotions. This language factor causes untold difficulty in speaking clearly about morality. It seems preferable to reserve terms such as immoral, sin, and guilty to the area of personal involvement where free and conscious decision-making comes into play.

Further, as concerned Christians, we should not remain content with the simple knowledge that ignorance, error or other so-called "excusing causes" have prevented individuals from arriving at correct moral judgments and that their actions do not constitute personal sinfulness. Guiltless actions frequently cause immense havoc in society and harm other persons. Unjustified warfare, racial prejudice, marital infidelity, or stealing from big businesses may have little moral culpability about them in some cases, but the carnage of warfare, indignities suffered, wrecked marriages, and lost investments bear eloquent testimony to the importance of promoting correct insights into moral values. Education in human and Christian moral values should aim at inculcating those freely accepted choices which fulfill man individually and socially in response to God.

By way of conclusion, the concrete moral judgment called conscience is more complex than we sometimes think. It refers not only to one's judgment about the proposed action, but also to one's person fulfillment. Realizing this important distinction, we may gain greater understanding, appreciation, and tolerance of certain reprehensible actions. An assassin murders a president; military leaders commit atrocities against civilians or kill prisoners; terrorists kill innocent people in the name of progress through revolution. A pathological personality or the hysteria of wartime reactions may blur the proper judgment of moral values. Admitting the erroneous nature of such judgments, we may nevertheless appreciate the personal goodness sometimes intended through these very acts. A person who makes an erroneous decision may, in fact, merit in God's estimation by responding according to his human capacities, for God always expects that we follow our personal judgment of conscience. It is, therefore, of paramount importance that we intend always to love God and our neighbor, striving always to answer God's calls in our activities, whatever be the actual inner or objective goodness of our actions.

Some Contemporary Approaches to Conscience

Like most other areas in theology, the question of conscience has undergone some rethinking and consequent adjustment in some aspects of this traditional doctrine explained previously. These new insights do not as such contradict the foregoing, but serve rather to complete the understanding we have of man's moral knowledge. These complementary notions may be viewed under several headings: the nature of connatural knowledge; the object of moral knowledge; conscience as inner harmony of the person; and conscience in a personalist or relational perspective.

1. *Connatural Knowledge.* In the previous pages, reference has been made to knowledge by connaturality. St. Thomas describes such knowledge in the following way: "The rightness of judgment can happen in a twofold way: in one way, through the perfect use of reason; in another way, by a certain connaturality to those matters which are to be judged; for example, a person who has learned moral knowledge (in a technical fashion) judges rightly through the inquiry of his reason about those matters which pertain to chastity; but the person who has the virtue of chastity judges rightly about the same matters through a certain connaturality to chastity" (*S.T.* II-II, q. 45, a. 2). Maritain comments about this kind of knowledge: "But we would have only a very incomplete picture of human knowledge if we did not take into account another type of knowledge, entirely different, which is not acquired through concepts and reasoning, but through *inclination,* as St. Thomas says, or through sympathy, congeniality or connaturality" (J. Maritain, *The Range of Reason* [1952] 16).

A growing awareness of the fact and nature of such knowledge prompts a number of theologians today to see abstract and systematic knowledge as a secondary and derived form of human knowledge. (See J. Glaser, "Authority, Connatural Knowledge, and the Spontaneous Judgment of the Faithful," *Theological Studies* 29 [1968] 742-51, esp. 746f., which has been used as the basis of this section.) Maritain will speak of conceptually formulated knowledge as "a kind of after-knowledge" and other authors stress that such reasoned knowledge should not be mistaken for the highest and purest form of human knowledge. Josef Fuchs distinguishes between a reflexive, conceptually formulated knowledge of moral realities (e.g., ethics or moral theology) and a richer primary knowledge which contains more than this reflexive formulation and is the very source of this secondary knowledge. Karl Rahner frequently utilizes the distinction between the "pre-conceptually known" and the "conceptually known" as a key theological distinction.

Fuchs recognizes the legitimacy of an intuitive application of universal moral principles to the concrete situation: "The application of universal laws is not necessarily made in an explicit manner; nor is there required an abstract and antecedent knowledge of *all* principles. For by an immediate understanding (they say: 'by intuition') the situation can be grasped under its moral aspect; this knowledge therefore is not so much a deductive knowledge *from* reasons, as rather based *in* reasons which have been grasped" (*Theologia moralis generalis,* pars prima, 154). Fuchs remarks further that an explicit philosophical-theological reflection should act as an instance of control and confirmation of such pre-conceptual knowledge. Both forms of knowledge, pre-conceptual and conceptual, must be ready to learn from one another. In a case of conflict we cannot say a priori which source of knowledge is right. Perhaps the supposedly genuine pre-conceptual knowledge is nothing more than a feeling and must be shown to be such by systematic reflection. Perhaps the system has to be overhauled in the light of new data, previously overlooked, and now presented through genuine pre-conceptual knowledge. The point is that the data offered us by genuine pre-conceptual knowledge deserve as serious consideration as the systematic reflection to which it might stand opposed.

K. Rahner describes in more detail the nature of this intuitive application of general moral principles to the concrete situation (See *The Dynamic Element in the Church* 13-41.) The context of his remarks concerns the person in the state of grace and open therefore to God's friendship. Such a person does not possess the same consciousness as the sinner or a person as yet in the immature state prior to his original and initial decision to choose God. (Rahner conjectures elsewhere that "probably the decision of faith which stamps one's total life occurs today as a rule somewhere between the ages of twenty and twenty-five"—quote by J. Glaser, "Man's Existence: Supernatural Partnership," *Theological Studies* 30 [1969] 473-88, at 474-75.) After this initial option, the person's existence is now a realized and accepted loving encounter with God. In this relationship, he finds his authentic freedom and experiences his birth as a true person. However unconceptualized this divine encounter might be, it constitutes the very heart or core of his consciousness. The form it takes in his consciousness will be more that of an experience of peace, hope, openness, than that of ideas and concepts dealing with God, transcendence, decision, and so forth. This primary or arche-consciousness serves a function analogous to that of the first principles of logic and philosophy. It is similar to these in that it is the norm against which the particular is measured. It is different from these because it serves this function on a pre-conceptual but highly intellectual level of consciousness. The person confronted with a concrete set of alternatives experiences the goodness or evil of an action as the pre-conceptual harmony or disharmony between what he is and is conscious of being (a freely accepted transcendence to the Infinite) and the concrete alternatives. The morally good, held in the light of the good he is and is conscious of being, harmonizes with this; it confirms, deepens, and corresponds to this fundamental peace, openness, tranquillity. The morally evil alternative, held in this realized transcendence, clashes with and contradicts this fundamental peace and light.

To draw a weak parallel: this is analogous to the kind of knowledge one has that a certain movement of music "fits" a larger piece of music in tone, color, movement, etc. One knows, for example, with dead certainty that a song by the Beatles does not "fit" anywhere in a Bach fugue—and this prior to any speculative reflection. The connatural knowledge we are speaking of is essentially different from this, of course; but such an example might be of some help in understanding its nature when contrasted with a reflexive speculation on the same matter. Might not the artist's grasp of the harmony of a painting, or the sculptor's sense of proportion serve as additional examples of this kind of "pre-conceptual" knowledge?

The existence of such pre-conceptual knowledge as a valid source of moral insight carries implications for our understanding of conscience. We cannot rule out in advance, for instance, that the individual Christian, working on the basis of pre-conceptually grasped moral insights, may conclude to concrete decisions which go beyond a minimum morality of law. We have stated this notion repeatedly and spoken of the inner guidance of the Holy Spirit as the primary source of moral knowledge for the faithful Christian. Is not the notion of pre-conceptual knowledge a technical way of stating how the individual person grasps this guidance? The saints, for instance, often spoke of a certainty in heroic activity (e.g., martyrdom, spending themselves in the service of others) which preceded rational argumentation. On the other hand, we cannot preclude the possibility of the faithful person gaining pre-conceptual moral insight into a valid alternative for him which contradicts the universal moral law as previously formulated (e.g., this may be the case in the matter of birth regulation). When a considerable number of Christian faithful share such spontaneous moral judgments, it should weigh heavily in favor of a reconsideration of the traditionally formulated moral norm. (There is a sense, then, in which Fletcher's contention about "the loving person doing the loving thing" has a certain validity. For this reason, we opted for the "combination form" of Frankena's four options concerning the relation between charity and norms. This allows for the fact that, at times, fresh insights in the concrete situation will permit the individual, conscientious person to judge rightly that a previously articulated moral norm should be applied to the case at hand and that he should opt for a contrary solution. Unlike Fletcher, however, we have accepted the possibility of formulating some universal moral norms which will find application in all conceivable cases. We do not "make up our rules" as we enter each new situation.)

From this technical explanation of connatural knowledge as stemming from the inner depths of the person, moreover, one can understand better why theologians such as Häring, Monden, and Colavechio will speak of conscience as preceding any division of man's faculties of intellect and will. The prime reality of conscience as man's moral awareness is man's deepest self-consciousness. These authors present conscience in terms of personal development "not as an intellectual conclusion, nor as a motivating influence on the will, but rather as a harmonious production of man's personality" (X. Colavechio, "Conscience: A Personalist Perspective," *Continuum* 5 [1967] 203-10, at 204.) The inner harmony or disharmony which a person experiences between his awareness of who he is, in all his vital relationships, and the manifestation of this awareness by his chosen action constitutes conscience in its deepest sense. At this profound level of man's being, his awareness of choosing what fulfills him authentically as a person creates a sense of harmonious unity. The experience of a so-called bad conscience may be viewed as a profound rift in the depths of man's being, leading to a sense of disunity in one's self. Conscience thus implies man's sense of authenticity and unauthenticity.

2. *The Object of Moral Knowledge.* The approach to moral knowledge outlined previously distinguishes between two aspects of the one act of conscience: (a) the judgment about the objective morality of the proposed action; (b) the judgment about personal fulfillment through this action. This approach has been criticized at times for the following reasons among others.

The traditional approach emphasizes an understanding of the moral life as a series of isolated actions. Man seems to choose freely and consciously with great frequency. A contemporary understanding would stress more the life-direction, -tendency, or -orientation which the person chooses. This tendency stems from the inmost core of the person and becomes manifest in the various concrete choices he makes. In a primary sense, therefore, some authors do not see the person as choosing individual "objects," traditionally termed the "matter" of one's free choices. They consider that the traditional approach leaves this "matter" as "something out there" which the person takes to himself. Man knows and wills matter, but this "matter" seems too abstract and apart from himself. The danger exists therefore of constituting a world of things (the matter of one's actions) and considering these things in themselves. This may well have been the underlying problem which led to the former tendency to absolutize morality to an excessive extent. If one can pin down realities such as lying, theft, or sexual conduct as a "thing," which the person grasps or takes to himself, then one can construct a prefabricated code morality which takes little account of the circumstances involved in concrete situations. "An act of moral freedom is not so much a choice of something outside the person which God wants the individual to choose; rather it is an act of self-creation, an act which has as its object the free person himself. . . . Moral cognition terminates primarily not in some object outside the subject; rather it is a consciousness of the subject himself as possibility, as absolutely necessary possibility" (J. Glaser, "Transition between Grace and Sin: Fresh Perspectives," *Theological Studies* 29 [1968] 260-74, at 267). J. Metz writes:

> With the growing insight into man's original manner of being, into his subjectivity, it becomes ever clearer that his powers terminate not in some object but in man himself. . . . Therefore neither does his freedom occur merely as an object-orientated engagement, as a choice "between" individual objects, but rather as self-realization of the individual who chooses objects, and only within this freedom, in which one "produces himself," is he also "free" with regard to the material of his self-realization. He can do this or that or omit it with respect to his own (indispensable) self-realization (quoted by Glaser, 267).

In a real sense, therefore, the prime object of man's freedom and moral knowledge is himself, the free individual in all his here-and-now concreteness, the individual as God-given task. This fits in with the notion of natural law explained previously.

Natural law connotes man's task to discern and fulfill the implications of his full, personal being. We have seen that man's being-a-man includes not only the universal characteristics he shares with other men, but also those unique, individuating characteristics possessed by this person alone. This fullness of the person's being is the created means or instrument in which God communicates himself and in which God's offering of himself realizes itself. Bruno Schüller writes in this vein:

> The law of God, as far as content is concerned, is the man himself, as he is offered himself, not only in his membership in a community, but also in his multiple other social relationships, and not least of all is his unique individuality. So the law of God demands of the individual that he be himself (quoted by Glaser, 268).

These insights summarized in Glaser's articles have practical implications, for they imply a different way of determining the seriousness or slightness of "matter" (i.e., the objective content of the moral act). By viewing the object of freedom and moral knowledge as "something out there," the object of choice assumes a great deal of unchangeableness and does not relate intimately to the individual performing the act. Glaser stresses that, since the object of moral choice always relates to the fullness of *this* person's developing being, the object of choice shares this developmental and changing character. In traditional categories, for example, infant masturbation would have the same *objective* meaning, hence the same objective deordination, as masturbation in adulthood. Moralists have suspected and stated the wrongness of such a conclusion. The recent approach to the object of choice and moral knowledge as being the person himself in all his concreteness and relationships permits one to give a better theological explanation of such cases. The nature of the infant or child simply does not at his stage of growth constitute an adequate medium for a personal response to God's call. "Just because such a dimension of man as nature—e.g., his sexuality—in its fullest stage of development is capable of being the medium of God's self-communication in its fullest form and intensity, a call to the very core of the person, does it necessarily follow that it must be so in all stages of its development on the way to this final stage? Is it not conceivable that just as the dimension of nature itself grows and deepens, so too does its ability to be the medium of this ultimate call of and encounter with God? And is it not possible that until it reaches a certain intensity of development, it is still on its way to this final stage and might be experienced as obligation, as a possible area of self-realization and hence encounter with God, but to a lesser degree than this ultimate fundamental encounter it will later have?" (Glaser, 269-70). Whereas the more traditional view would understand masturbation by a child to have diminished or removed responsibility because of lessened freedom and knowledge, this more recent view would not see the child's nature (the object of his moral choices) as serving capably as a medium of ultimate encounter with God. The child has simply not attained such development in his nature, and since "serious matter" implies that the proposed object of moral choice *can* serve as a medium of ultimate encounter leading to full commitment to or rejection of God, no "serious matter" ever presents itself to the child. The development of the person's nature throughout adolescence will include not only his physical maturation, but also those other dimensions which make up the person as a moral reality and involve all the richness which constitutes the totality of genuine personal being: physical, emotional, intellectual, social, and psychological.

This approach does not destroy the objectivity of morality, but it does represent a significant shift in emphasis and it has important consequences in assessing the meaning of human actions and consequently their gravity. (See R. McCormick, "Notes on Moral Theology," *Theological Studies* 29 [1968] 684f.) The example given above about masturbation by infants or children could easily be extended to the question of adolescent masturbation. Does the adolescent's nature constitute a medium capable of serving as a created medium of an ultimate encounter with God? Besides raising practical consequences regarding age-categories, moreover, we may ask whether the same line of reasoning would find application in analyzing the morality of entire peoples. Might a primitive tribe or men of another era have a "nature," understood as their unique fullness of being in biocultural and social conditions, considerably different from that of twentieth-century Americans in general? Does their nature serve necessarily in certain questions as an insufficient medium for an ultimate encounter with God? Definite answers cannot be given to such intriguing speculations. They do, however, merit serious reflection.

It seems worthwhile to close this section with some words of K. Rahner and H. Vorgrimler on the development and stages of man's history and our attitude thereto:

> Each phase of life (childhood, youth, etc., and their different characteristics) has its own irreplaceable originality and hence its own role to play: to raise itself to the next phase and to integrate itself there as an abiding element. With this is set before us an eminently religious task, for the individual . . . as well as the educator, and above all for the theologian. The task is to work out the differences which the various phases of life produce in their existential relationship to Christian truths and to the individual moral goal-commandments. . . . A failure to recognize such findings results in speaking to Christians in an unselective, undifferentiated, and schematic way. This overburdens them and like every ironbound legalism can end in a casting off of religion altogether. As long as deeper insight into these phases of life is lacking, a genuinely understood Christian patience can go a long way to help to allow time for the development of the individual—even in the religious sphere. So too can love, which accepts another even then as a Christian and brother when he has not (yet) arrived at the goal of all commands and matters pertaining to the Church (quoted by J. Glaser, *Theological Studies* 29 [1968] 273-74).

3. *Conscience in a Personalist Perspective.* Reference has been made in the previous pages of recent tendencies to view conscience as a profound depth of the person and to abandon an overly essentialistic understanding of man in favor of emphasizing the individual person in his concreteness and personal relationships. Many contemporaries see authentic personhood as emerging only in man's free acceptance of himself in his vital relationships to other persons and ultimately to God. Man-in-relationship, therefore, constitutes an oft-repeated theme of contemporary philosophy and theology.

In his article "Conscience: A Personalist Perspective" (*Continuum* 5 [1967] 203-10), Xavier G. Colavechio applies these insights to the question of conscience. He views the human person as standing at the convergence of his principal relationships in all their concreteness. Thus, his relationships to his family, friends, enemies, customers, or to his creator become main factors in grasping who *this* person really is. In a real sense, the individual person is the sum total of these relationships, taken in their ontological sense. The person's assumption of the implications of these relationships for his moral conduct, his *awareness* of what these relationships should mean for his moral choices, is a dynamic and progressive reality, for the relationships which have a certain stability (e.g., to his family) develop as the person matures and passes through the various life-stages. Other relationships have a more casual and transitory character (e.g., to fellow workers or neighbors). Fundamental to all the person's relationships as a Christian is, however, his relation to Christ and to the people of God gathered in Christ.

Applying these notions to conscience, Colavechio sees it as a "tension between his awareness of himself as he is and the manifestation of this awareness by his chosen action." The consequent disharmony and rift within oneself cries out for healing; this cry is conscience. The inmost sense of harmony resulting from a correlation between one's awareness of himself and one's chosen action, on the other hand, likewise stems from the voice of conscience. Moral certitude for the individual is dependent on the awareness of his unique relationships and his personal awareness of the demands that these relationships make upon him. If a person has seriously pondered all his relationships (e.g., to his girlfriend, his parents) and the effects of his choices upon these relationships (e.g., his choice to marry his girlfriend may cause his parents great displeasure), if he has at least implicitly tried to arrive at the ontological reality which underlies these relationships, and with this information arrives at a decision which he carries out, he follows his conscience. A constant communication process, whether in the family, in school, or in the Church, brings the person to an ever-growing awareness of the ontological relationships which obtain in his life and to the implications these relationships hold for his ethical conduct as a follower of Christ. He becomes aware of himself as *this* person possessing a unique character and called in a special way, for he alone has *his* relationships.

This approach complements the explanations given above. It has the merit of avoiding an over-objectification of morality in a world of things; it stresses rather a world of persons in their relationships. It permits insight into such practical moral failings as lying, stealing, or sexual misconduct: instead of making these choices "things," it views them as violations of personal values and, ultimately, of the inherent dignity of the other person. Tied in with Glaser's stress on the object of moral choice as man himself in his uniqueness and concrete relationships, moreover, this personalist approach surpasses readily the traditional tendency toward a law-centered and hence exteriorized "code-morality." Moral values and moral misconduct become intimately linked with the interiority of the human person, in that core of personal being where a person is most truly himself and master of his choices. This fits well our basic notion of natural law and the Pauline ethic: "Become what you already are." Colavechio's article does not spell out in detail many practical applications of this personalized understanding of morality and conscience. He has, however, performed the service of presenting a framework within which our theological reflections may develop.

THE FORMATION OF CONSCIENCE

The developing and sharpening of conscience should concern every person called in Christ. Christian moral life consists in responsiveness to conscience in a free and conscious fashion. How can the person accurately respond, if he does not accurately hear God's call in the depths of his own being? Sufficient knowledge mixed with a mature sense of Christian freedom should be the goal of the morally aware Christian. Attention should be given not just to negative obligations (how to avoid sins), but to positive moral values (how to develop the open-ended character of Christian love). A sincere and diligent conscientiousness, proportionate to the matter at hand and in keeping with one's talents and state in life, should characterize the mature Christian. The sensitivity of an upright conscience should not be confused with scrupulous anxiety.

Conscience develops normally under the influence of the morally significant impressions gained in human experience from birth onward. The judgments, standards and values of beloved persons, such as parents, become incorporated internally with the gradual development of the child's personality. The authoritarian and legal strictures of the youthful conscience should progress in time from being an external disciplinary agent to an independent position of free response to personal appreciation of moral value. Defects in normal psychological development can result in distorted malfunctionings which interfere or inhibit an authentic moral sense. Pastoral literature frequently refers to instances of such retarded growth under various headings: fixation, regression to earlier stages of development, unhealthy guilt feelings, transference of guilt, compulsive and obsessive anxiety. At times, too, there can develop a total lack of conscientious response, sometimes called moral insanity. Intelligence may remain intact, yet there exists a psychopathic lack of the vital affective element of conscience which bears the person to embrace the moral value which he grasps intellectually. This seems the case of the so-called sociopath. (See the articles of D. McCarthy, W. Weisner, R. Campbell, and G. Shattuck in *Conscience: Its Freedom and Limitations,* ed. W. Bier, 39-98.)

The proper development of conscience depends greatly on moral instruction, especially through formal and informal religious education, both at home and at school. Children first acquire their moral awareness largely from social adaptation through example, praise, and punishment. The aim of moral education touches not only the extent of moral knowledge at one's command, but also the freedom, independence and due autonomy the person brings to bear in his moral judgments and choices, together with their depth, intensity, and vitality. The example of an authentic Christian life in the family and a gentle step-by-step guidance in response to a loving God (not the Supreme Lawmaker) will permit children to see and to love freely moral values. Such values will not be coercively imposed from without, but seen rather as the fullness of being-a-man. Correction and punishment should be accompanied by explanations of the intrinsic nature of the wrongdoing, and God should not be depicted as the Judge in fiery wrath or the Tyrant who hates little children. "It's wrong because I told you so" as the typical parental explanation will hardly convey the dignity of a son's response to God's loving calls to love him and one's neighbors.

The Christian formation of conscience should inculcate a certain opportunity of adopting a personal point of view and an independence free from the undue interference of other persons or the overriding influence of irrational psychological forces. The adult Christian conscience does not depend on the mass movements of the moment, which may verge at times on mass hysteria, on the pressure of family influence and parental value-systems, or on an externally imposed code-morality. Self-conviction, not the following of the herd, is the ultimate goal of moral education. God calls each man by his own name and not by another's. Each person should be encouraged to experience the joy of genuine Christian freedom. (See M. Oraison, *Love or Constraint?* [Paramus, N.J.: Paulist Press, 1959], which explains many psychological aspects of religious education.)

NORMS AND CONSCIENCE

The moral norms formulated through the experience of past and present Christian reflection on the implications of Jesus' Word provide an abundant source for concrete moral judgments. As has been mentioned, we are keenly aware today of the need to take a hard look at some absolute, negative, universal norms formulated by previous generations of Christians. This does not, however, destroy the presumption in favor of applying directly many such insights. Often enough, such norms mirror the inherent dignity proper to the human person conformed to the image of Christ. Isn't this a consequence of taking natural law doctrine seriously? Moral norms rightly articulated express the deep tendency of love produced in us by the Holy Spirit. They spell out in some details the implications of discipleship for the individual. They state in universal terms what God asks of man in situations which have the same morally relevant features, e.g., that it is always forbidden to commit infanticide or to calumniate another person. Conscience draws on these norms as expressions of the moral life to which we are called in Christ. These norms articulate the deepest urgings of man's personal being, if they are correctly formulated. By personally appropriating these formulations handed down in Christian experience, the individual Christian can avoid mere caprice in moral judgments and an overly arbitrary approach to concrete decisions. Vatican II mentions the need of such norms explicitly:

> The more that a correct conscience holds sway, the more persons and groups turn aside from blind choice and strive to be guided by objective norms of morality. Conscience frequently errs from invincible ignorance without losing its dignity. The same cannot be said of a man who cares but little for truth and goodness, or of a conscience which by degrees grows practically sightless as a result of habitual sin (*Pastoral Constitution on the Church in the Modern World,* n. 16).

Conscience and Authority

External authorities can never replace one's personal conscience. God expects me to follow *my* conscience, not someone else's. The greatest problem posed in this context for Catholics is the proper weight to be accorded to pronouncements of Church authorities. To accept in theory the inviolability of personal conscience differs enormously from the practical application of this doctrine to actual decisions. Vatican II warns clearly: "Let the layman not imagine that his pastors are always such experts, that to every problem which arises, however complicated, they can readily give him a concrete solution, or even that such is their mission" (*Pastoral Constitution on the Church in the Modern World,* n. 43). The fact remains, however, that many Catholics fail to assume the authentic personal responsibility which is their Christian heritage. Preaching and teaching the Word should urge the individual's rights and duties in this regard.

The truly authoritative teaching office of the Church never-theless occupies a central role in the formation of Christian con-science. The guidance of the Holy Spirit assists in a special way the entire Christian community to gain progressive insight into the implications of the Gospel announced in Christ. Aware of this divine assistance, the believing Catholic will listen openly and attentively to the pope and the college of bishops when they proclaim the community's faith. Their vital role of uniting and guiding the ecclesial body will instill in the faithful a willingness to listen, a docility, and a presumption that adequate expression of the moral implications of Christ's message is being communi-cated. Such openness and docility should not be construed as a servile abandonment of personal responsibility, but rather as a due acknowledgment of Christ's presence in his ecclesial body. Some words of Vatican II speak to this point:

> In the formation of their consciences, the Christian faithful ought carefully to attend to the sacred and certain doctrine of the Church. The Church is, by the will of Christ, the teacher of truth. It is her duty to give utterance to, and authoritatively to teach, that truth which is Christ himself, and also to declare and confirm by her authority those principles of the moral order which have their origin in human nature itself" (*Dec-laration on Religious Freedom,* n. 14. See also chapters I and VIII for additional treatment of material pertaining to the magisterium and conscience. A. Dulles, "The Contemporary Magisterium," *Theology Digest* 17 [1969] 299-311, provides an up-to-date treatment of the main principles underlying this question today. C. Curran, "Church Law and Conscience," *in A New Look at Christian Morality,* 125-43, will also prove helpful).

THE RIGHT TO FOLLOW PERSONAL CONSCIENCE

Man fulfills himself by following his personal conscience. Without doubt, the free formation and following of conscience constitute fundamental human rights. To harm these rights in-jures the person gravely, for it attacks the deepest level of his self. Catholic doctrine states well the American consciousness of this basic right:

Man perceives and acknowledges the imperative of the divine law through the mediation of conscience. In all his activity a man is bound to follow his conscience faithfully, in order that he may come to God, for whom he was created. It follows that he is not to be forced to act in a manner contrary to his conscience. Nor, on the other hand, is he to be restrained from acting in accordance with his conscience, especially in matters religious (*Declaration on Religious Freedom,* n. 3).

Interference with the proper formation of conscience cannot be condemned too strongly. The teaching of errors may lead another to live his moral life totally outside the proper path. The inculcation of racial or class hatred, religious indifference, belligerent attitudes toward other countries, atheism, sexual promiscuity and the like are thoroughly reprehensible, even though the propagators of such teachings are sometimes personally inculpable. A graver responsibility falls on those who of set purpose propose immoral practices under the guise of virtue or other deceptions, for example, by leading children to steal or to commit illicit sexual actions. Especially in the more impressionable years including adolescence, such example or teachings may instill lifelong habits which will prove difficult to uproot in adulthood. Vatican II reiterated pertinent Catholic doctrine in this area also:

This holy synod likewise affirms that children and young people have a right to be encouraged to weigh moral values with an upright conscience, and to embrace them by personal choice, and to know and love God more adequately. Hence, it earnestly entreats all who exercise government over peoples or preside over the work of education to see that youth is never deprived of this sacred right. It urges sons of the Church to devote themselves generously to the whole enterprise of education, with the special aim of helping to bring more speedily to all men everywhere the worthy benefits of education and training (*Declaration on Christian Education,* n. 2).

Proper respect and reverence should always be paid to a person who follows his conscience, even if he unknowingly errs. St. Paul taught this Christian attitude in his letters to the Romans and Corinthians in relation to the "weak" who remain doubtful about the lawfulness of eating certain foods. He warns them that charity should lead Christians to avoid actions which would scandalize the weak (Romans 14:10f.; 1 Cor. 8:9-13). Another facet of the apostle's teaching commands attention: no one should accommodate his own conscience to the erroneous conscience of his neighbor (Rom. 14:22). A person in error cannot expect that others acknowledge and follow his views. (See T. B. Maston, *Biblical Ethics* [Cleveland: World Pub. Co., 1967] 179.)

Every person has the right to follow his personal conscience. This general principle needs explanation and accurate application in some complicated cases, but it finds its roots in God's Word. St. Peter defends this right of conscience. in the case of an upright conscience before the judge who forbids preaching about Christ (Acts 5:29). The Church's official teaching has explicitly upheld this right and obligation in forbidding anyone to be forced to profess the Catholic faith against his conscience.

> Religious freedom . . . means that all men are to be immune from coercion on the part of individuals or social groups and of any human power, in such wise that in matters religious no one is to be forced to act in a manner contrary to his own beliefs. Nor is anyone to be restrained from acting in accordance with his own beliefs, whether privately or publicly, whether alone or in association with others, within due limits (*Declaration on Religious Freedom,* n. 2).

This right to follow one's conscience can never be impeded through thought control, brainwashing, and the like. These would constitute violations of man's personal dignity. But does a person have an unlimited right to follow his personal conscience in the carrying out of all his external actions? For instance, can a person who professes to act in good conscience or from religious motives murder, steal, take his own life or perform bodily harm to another? The example of the Jehovah's Witnesses comes to mind in this context: can parents be obliged to allow a blood transfusion for their children, even though they view this as contrary to their religious tenets? American legal codes do not permit these kinds of following of personal conscience, for they violate the established rights of other people or create grave social harm.

Christian moral principles arrive at a similar conclusion. Some traditional moral guidelines come into play in this context. These principles do not provide hard-and-fast answers for all possible instances and human prudence must assess the concrete situations. These principles do, however, give insight into some suggested procedures for resolving difficulties in this area.

First, a person who follows his erroneous conscience without injuring others should not be prevented from acting, unless he objects unreasonably against his own welfare, as in the prevention of suicide or grave self-mutilation or injury to one's health. A number of practical examples come to mind. Could not bystanders prevent a person protesting the Vietnam war from taking his life by setting himself afire, as actually happened before the United Nations Building in New York? Could not parents or society prevent children and adolescents from taking heroin or LSD? These actions may well be judged as unreasonable and irresponsible by society at large. In such instances, the socially accepted standards of morality seem to mirror the Christian standards enunciated in our formulations of the natural law. Genuine self-fulfillment, for example, will never involve suicide, for the individual's personal being possesses a basic tendency toward self-preservation. Prevention of suicide may allow the person to gain an opportunity to grasp more accurately the direction of his authentic self-fulfillment.

Second, a person who follows his erroneous conscience and injures others should be prevented from performing his external deed. His internal conscience must, of course, be respected, but one need not permit him to accomplish his harmful conduct. One could try to explain this restraint of another's action on the basis of a supposed clash of rights. Thus, the person in erroneous conscience who injures others through his actions retains his right to his internal conscience, some will say, but the right of other persons, founded on truth, prevails in the external order. Many theologians in the past have based their explanations of this problem on this theory of a clash or collision of rights or duties. It seems preferable, however, to say simply that the person in error has no right whatsoever to injure other people. It is not a matter of his right ceding to a stronger right; it is rather a case of one right, the right of the other persons to their own welfare, founded on the one virtue of justice. Though on the surface we see only a clash of distinct rights, further analysis and reflection view the moral order as one and the superficial distinctness of rights disappears.

Many practical consequences follow from this view. For instance, a person in erroneous conscience has no unlimited right to sell pornography, to steal for a supposedly worthy cause, to foment revolution, or to perjure himself in court. These actions have social repercussions which civil authorities may lawfully impede. In preventing such actions performed in good conscience, the State safeguards the common welfare of its citizens. Laws prohibiting pornography, prostitution, polygamy, and the like may be justified under this heading.

The civil authorities may justifiably decide, on the other hand, that toleration of such abuses may at times be better. Such decisions may be based on the conviction that the total suppression of immoral or reprehensible practices by laws may lead to graver evils. For this reason, many jurisdictions tolerate carefully regulated prostitution, divorce, and lascivious entertainment. In such cases, the civil authorities do not necessarily approve or encourage these practices, but rather allow them to continue as a means of avoiding more serious difficulties. The statement of the Catholic bishops of New York State, in which they spoke out several years ago with regret in favor of the widening of the grounds for divorce, should be understood in light of this principle. The question has also been raised concerning the abortion laws currently in effect. Must the State uphold the moral order with strict abortion laws? Or could the State allow greater breadth for the judgment of individual consciences? If a public consensus about the morality of abortion in more instances than those permitted by the civil laws gradually emerges in a clear fashion, then it will be most difficult to project the retention of the abortion laws currently in effect in many jurisdictions.

Third, one may not morally coerce or persuade another to act against his conscience. This does not exclude attempts to persuade another to *change* his judgment by offering him new arguments. The principle does imply, however, that if a person remains convinced of a certain course of action despite all argument to the contrary, he should follow this conviction and not be impeded. To induce him to do otherwise, especially by force, would be to lead him into sin. This holds true even for the case when we ourselves or society in general claim some right to external actions from a person in erroneous conscience, when his conscience judges that he cannot perform the action.

The entire question of conscientious objection comes under this last heading. Can the government force a person to fight in Vietnam or in any war when his conscience tells him this is immoral? Can the civil authorities force him through threat of imprisonment to participate in what he believes to be an unjust war? The bishops at Vatican II touched on the general treatment to be accorded conscientious objectors:

> It seems right that laws make humane provisions for the case of those who for reasons of conscience refuse to bear arms, provided, however, that they accept some other form of service to the human community (*Pastoral Constitution on the Church in the Modern World,* n. 79).

"The Constitution is careful in its statement of concern in this passage. The text makes no judgment on the objective moral claim of the conscientious objector. It neither accepts nor rejects the arguments in support of such a position. It simply appeals in the name of equity for humane treatment under the law of those who experience difficulties of conscience with respect to bearing arms" (W. Abbot-J. Gallagher, *The Documents of Vatican II,* footnote to text). Without judging the objective moral claim of conscientious objectors against warfare in general or against specific wars, (e.g., Vietnam), we would add, it seems immoral to coerce conscientious objectors through threat of imprisonment to fight against their conscience. Governments should make humane provisions for all conscientious objectors, including the so-called selective conscientious objectors who object only to particular wars and not to all war in general. If governments do not allow due provisions and instead imprison conscientious objectors, they act wrongly. The American bishops' statement on this question deserves full quotation:

The present laws of this country . . . provide only for those whose reasons of conscience are grounded in a total rejection of the use of military force. This form of conscientious objection deserves the legal provision made for it, but we consider that the time has come to urge that similar consideration be given those whose reasons of conscience are more personal and specific.

We therefore recommend a modification of the Selective Service Act making it possible, although not easy, for so-called selective conscientious objectors to refuse—without fear of imprisonment or loss of citizenship—to serve in wars which they consider unjust or in branches of service (e.g., the strategic nuclear forces) which would subject them to the performance of actions contrary to deeply held moral convictions about indiscriminate killing. Some other form of service to the human community should be required of those so exempted.

Whether or not such modifications in our laws are in fact made, we continue to hope that, in the all-important issue of war and peace, all men will follow their consciences. We can do no better than to recall, as did the Vatican Council, "the permanent binding force of universal natural law and its all embracing principles," to which "man's conscience itself gives ever more emphatic voice" (*Human Life in Our Day,* Nov. 15, 1968).

Conscientious objectors should not be presumed to act with insincerity, culpability, or cowardice. The peace movement today contains many individuals who are honestly attempting to follow their consciences, and the government should safeguard their rights, instead of prosecuting them as criminals. As Christians, we can but applaud sincere adherence to personal conviction based on conscience. The personal anguish and suffering brought into the lives of many conscientious objectors and their families bear eloquent testimony to their sincerity and belies the accusations hurled against them.

BIBLIOGRAPHY

Bier, W. (ed.), *Conscience: Its Freedom and Limitations* (N.Y.: Fordham Univ., 1971).

Böckle, F., *Fundamental Concepts of Moral Theology* (Paramus, N.J.: Paulist Press, 1968) 67-78.

Carpentier, R., "Conscience," *Dictionnaire de spiritualité ascetique et mystique,* II, 1459-575.

——, "Comment formuler le probleme de la conscience chrétienne?" *Problemi scelti di teologia contemporanea. Analecta Gregoriana,* Vol. 78 (Rome: Gregorian University, 1954) 463-68.

Chollet, A., "Conscience," *Dictionnaire de théologie catholique,* III, 1156-74.

Colavechio, X., *Erroneous Conscience and Obligations* (Wash., D.C.: Catholic University of America, 1961).

——, "Conscience: A Personalist Perspective," *Continuum* 5 (1967) 203-10.

Coulson, J., "The Authority of Conscience," *Downside Review* 77 (1959) 141-58.

Crowe, M., "The Term Synderesis and the Scholastics," *Irish Theological Quarterly* 23 (1956) 151-64, 228-45.

Curran, C., "Church Law and Conscience," *A New Look at Christian Morality* (Notre Dame: Fides, 1968) 125-43.

D'Arcy, E., *Conscience and Its Right to Freedom* (N.Y.: Sheed and Ward, 1961).

Dedek, J., "Some Moral Minimalism," *Chicago Studies* 7 (1968) 115-25.

Delhaye, P., The *Christian Conscience* (N.Y.: Desclée, 1968).

Dietz, D., "Conscience and Love," *American Ecclesiastical Review* 146 (1962) 225-32.

Doherty, R., *The Judgments of Conscience and Prudence* (River Forest, Ill., 1961).

Fuchs, J., *Theologia moralis generalis,* pars prima (Rome: Gregorian University, 1965) 151-218.

Glaser, J., "Authority, Connatural Knowledge, and the Spontaneous Judgment of the Faithful," *Theological Studies* 29 (1968) 742-751.

——, "Man's Existence: Supernatural Partnership," *Theological Studies* 30 (1969) 473-88.

——, "Transition between Grace and Sin: Fresh Perspectives," *Theological Studies* 29 (1968) 260-74.

Häring, B., *The Law of Christ,* Vol. I (Paramus, N.J.: Newman, 1961) 135-88.

————, "Moral Theology. Moral Systems," *Sacramentum Mundi* 4 (N.Y.: Herder & Herder, 1969) 130-33.

Hofmann, R., "Conscience," *Sacramentum Mundi* 1 (N.Y.: Herder and Herder, 1968) 411-14.

Kleinz, J., "Vatican II on Religious Freedom," *The Catholic Lawyer* 13 (1967) 180-97.

Lottin, O., *Morale Fondamentale* (Paris: Desclée, 1954) 163-65, 221-23, 324-39.

McDonagh, E., "The Theology of Conscience," in *Morals, Law and Authority* (Dayton: Pflaum Press, 1969) 115-26.

McKenzie, J., "Conscience," in *Dictionary of the Bible* (Milwaukee: Bruce, 1965).

Madden, J., "The Law of Charity and the Role of Conscience," *Australasian Catholic Record* 42 (1965) 308-15.

Monden, L., *Sin, Liberty, and Law* (N.Y.: Sheed & Ward, 1965).

Oraison, M., *Love or Constraint?* (Paramus, N.J.: Paulist Press, 1959).

Pierce, C., *Conscience in the New Testament* (London: SCM Press, 1955).

Schnackenburg, R., *The Moral Teaching of the New Testament* (N.Y.: Herder & Herder, 1965) 287-96.

St. John, H., "Toleration and Conscience," *Catholic Mind* 60 (1965) 51-58.

10. Christian Responsibility

"Let us make man in our own image, in the likeness of ourselves, and let them be masters . . . God created man in the image of himself, in the image of God he created him, male and female he created them. God blessed them, saying to them, 'Be fruitful, multiply, fill the earth and conquer it' " (Gen. 1:26-28). Man's personal activity in knowledge and freedom permits him to share the divine dominion in the world. How does man properly exercise this openness to transcend himself and to dispose of himself in his total being before God, men, and the world? What are the limits of his knowledge and freedom? A preliminary presentation of some traditional notions will guide our further inquiry.

THE APPROACH OF CLASSICAL MORAL THEOLOGY

Traditional moral theology of the past several centuries constructed a treatise "on human acts" which continues to govern much thinking in this area. Since this approach continues to exercise considerable influence, it will be useful to mention some prominent themes at the outset and show how they contrast with, are integrated into, or are complemented by more modern approaches.

The classical theologians present the individual acts of man as means of choosing his ultimate end, God. This *ethic of finality* views man's life as a series of choices of intermediate goals which have moral value insofar as they conform to the divine law. The ultimate norm of morality is seen as the Eternal Law, the divine plan or order for the world and man. This norm is mirrored in man's nature in the so-called Natural Law, which permits man to participate freely in the Eternal Law. The divine precepts of the Old and New Testaments constitute a more explicit, formulated source of man's moral duties. All duly promulgated human laws, civil and ecclesiastical, likewise articulate in more detailed fashion the moral norm. By conforming himself to these norms, which find their ultimate basis in the essence of God manifested more concretely in the Word made flesh, the person acts morally and becomes virtuous.

This traditional approach tends understandably to a *law-centeredness*, for "norm" connotes a measure for action. Man's moral activity is analyzed in terms of man's knowledge of the law and the extent of his freedom in conforming or not conforming to the demands inherent in it. A human act may thus be defined as an act which proceeds from man's free will with at least implicit advertence to the norm of morality. Such properly human activity differs from sub-human actions performed by men, but without the distinctively human qualities of knowledge and freedom, for example, the acts of a madman assassin, or the adventures of a sleep-walker.

The classical presentation, moreover, utilized a *facultative view of man*, emphasizing a notion of the moral act as flowing from man's faculties of intellect and will. The emotions were generally viewed as hindrances to the full use of freedom. The stress fell on man as rational. Within this context, *freedom* is seen as man's power of choosing through his will between objects which the intellect has grasped. This power of free choice seems realizable in its fullness rather easily, according to the disposition of the person. The fullness of freedom in any single act, therefore, was viewed as readily within the person's capabilities and it could then be generally presumed. Similarly, the *knowledge* needed for fully human activity concerned man's ability to discern the essential requirements of God's laws, whether the natural law, divine positive laws (as in the ten commandments), or human laws, both ecclesiastical and civil. This sort of discernment could occur in most men from the age of reason onward, perhaps even as early as the age of seven.

The traditional approach, finally, might accurately be termed an *act-moral,* insofar as it concentrated on the individual acts of the person and not on the person himself, who determines and shapes his life-orientation through his acts. Man's individual choices to this-or-that occupy more attention for the classical theologians than does his fundamental choice for-or-against God and man.

Modern moral theology has not entirely abandoned this traditional understanding of man and his free acts. Different emphases and considerable nuancing have, however, brought complementary ideas to the forefront.

THE APPROACH OF CONTEMPORARY MORAL THEOLOGY

The theme of responsibility has emerged as a unifying and central principle in contemporary religious ethics. This notion furnishes a new framework or structure for doing Christian ethics today. "Man as responder" has one task: "Be responsible!" God calls each person to respond to him by responding to the values, needs, and persons within the real world of his experience. The moral response is at the same time a religious response, for each responsible act directed to the ordering and bettering of the world is in answer to God's call, command, action, summons. The human person—graced, justified, and redeemed in Christ—hears God's Word in the world itself, a world in which man completes God's work. The world and Being, reconciled and elevated, root the divine call and man's response. Being is essentially the communion between God and man. (See A. Jonsen, *Responsibility in Modern Religious Ethics* [Washington: Corpus Books, 1968].)

The doctrine of natural law rests on this basic notion: God calls man through his personal being viewed concretely in all his relationships. All authentic human values of man-in-the-world find their ultimate basis in the creator. In the judgment of personal conscience, each individual seeks to discern these values and to realize them in his actions. The Christian sees charity as his primary value: being-there-for-others, as was Jesus Christ. To respect other people, to promote them, to serve them in their needs: this fulfills Christian responsibility. Responsibility means to employ the resources of discerning love in order to discover how the potentialities of Being can best be realized in accord with its exigencies.

This moral-religious response of the Christian takes shape through his free-choices, which manifest his fundamental stance or choice before men, the world, and God. In an entirely personal way, he reduces to practice the way of life manifested in his brother Jesus, thereby fulfilling his task of Christian responsibility.

This approach contrasts with that of classical moral theology. The ethic of responsibility—to God, to man, to the world—replaces a basically Aristotelian ethic with its emphasis on finality. Law serves man as related to fulfilling his own being; it does not compel as a foreign oppressor. The human person himself, in his deepest resources, not only his faculties of intellect and will, comes more prominently into the moral picture. As will be seen, knowledge and freedom assume a more profound significance when rooted in the depths of the person in his transcendence. The basic life-choice or fundamental option of the person likewise concerns the modern moralist to a more considerable extent than in the classical act-moral.

Using these notions, our challenge is to reconstruct a viable treatment on human activity. The following pages present some main elements of a new approach.

Man as Multidimensional Freedom

Many theologians today present a picture of man as multidimensional freedom. According to this view, man is structured in a series of concentric circles on various levels. On the deepest level of the individual, at the personal center or core of the self, man's original freedom decides, loves, commits itself in the fullest sense of these terms. On this level man constitutes himself as lover or selfish sinner. This is the center of grave morality where man makes himself and his total existence good or evil. An act originating in this dimension of man has the character of total and definitive disposition of self. Here, at the heart of the person, freedom engages itself with its fullest existential intensity. This act of core freedom translates time into eternity. When a completely free and decisive act occurs in absolute response to God's call or in a radical yes of love to another person, something eternal takes place. (See Glaser's articles in the bibliography of the preceding chapter for explanations of these themes; also J. Fuchs, "Basic Freedom and Morality," in *Human Values and Christian Morality*, 92-111.)

Freedom may thus be regarded as the fundamental unassailable ability of man to make personal the meaning of life. It is a basic condition for being a person, for it implies the individual's ability to dispose of himself in an irreducible fashion. This original freedom, unlike traditional ways of speaking about freedom, is not so much a faculty limited to choosing between various objects, as rather the radical capacity for accepting the appeal of one's personal transcendence. Personal freedom thus implies the ability to constitute one's own personality (personhood) as one called to go beyond oneself toward the world in knowledge and love. In this transcendence and dynamic orientation toward God, one grows into an authentic person, reaching beyond the limited boundaries of his given nature, thereby accepting the meaning of life. To refuse this gift of being-a-person means to stifle growth by selfishly turning from the world, from other persons, and, through this, from God. Moral evil ultimately means a person refuses himself. Only if he abandons himself to God does he receive himself back as his own personal possession. Original freedom is, then, the possibility of saying yes or no to oneself, the possibility of deciding for or against oneself.

This more radical meaning of human freedom figures prominently in the general philosophico-theological view of such theologians as Karl Rahner and Johannes Metz. Man has his fundamental relationship to God in his openness to Being as a whole. God supports all Being as its transcendent cause and may be termed its ground. In reaching out beyond oneself in transcendence, one experiences the unity of all Being in knowing and recognizing any particular being. How can one know this being, if one does not know Being as such? Knowledge of any particular being implies, therefore, knowledge of God himself, present as the mental horizon of which we become conscious in being conscious of finite realities. God is thus present in any human exercise of knowledge and freedom as the prior context. This has the very practical implication that in all human knowledge and freedom, man experiences God himself. In every free act, God is present, even though not grasped explicitly. Understood in these metaphysical terms, the God-experience refers to the silent, beckoning, yet withdrawing mystery at the frontiers of our experience of all reality. God is the horizon of life who remains always beyond reach, but toward whom we have a positive orientation in the depths of our being. (See J. Metz, "Freedom as a Threshold Problem between Philosophy and Theology," *Philosophy Today* 10 [1966] 264-79.)

In his sovereign freedom, the God of Love has approached us intimately and personally, communicating himself in his Word, Jesus Christ. This self-communication of God is most properly speaking grace, the gift of God himself. This relationship far exceeds our fundamental openness to God as Being. God offers himself as our direct possession in what has been traditionally called sanctifying grace. Human freedom thus receives an undue intimacy and an immediacy to God through which it becomes the radical power to say yes or no to God as he offers himself in free dialogue of the covenant. Man can, in other words, accept or reject the gratuitous self-communication of God and his offer of sonship and life in the Spirit. When freedom is thus seen as the free love of God in dialogue with the partner necessary to such freely given love, it appears as the essential dignity of the Christian person and all mankind.

The Fundamental Option

Because we are finite and historical, the expression of our transcendence and the personal disposal of ourselves occur over a lifetime and not in a single act. Individual actions and moral decisions lend a particular orientation of a life for or against God according to the seriousness whereby they engage our original freedom as persons. The radical capacity to say yes or no to God takes place through our personal exercise of transcendence by which we relate to God present at the horizon and as the intimate personal gift present in grace. This transcendence becomes realized through our relationships to the world of persons and things which surround us. In our attitudes and actions toward this world, we assume a basic stance toward God, who offers himself. Over a whole series of decisions and actions, we determine ourselves either as loving persons by accepting God's self-offer, or as people who reject God's appeal in favor of other appeals reaching us from men, the world, or our own selves. The source of any affirmative or negative choice toward God lies in the adoption of a right or wrong attitude toward the finite world of persons and things. Our love of the neighbor, for example, implies necessarily our love for God. Through and beyond the finite, we take a position toward God himself. This is the ultimate meaning of freedom as the power of transcendence: the self-achievement of the person using a finite material, before the infinite God. (See K. Rahner, "Reflections on the Unity of the Love of Neighbor and the Love of God," in *Theological Investigations,* Vol. VI, 231-49.)

Only to the extent, therefore, that this ultimate freedom penetrates our various "object-choices" (Monden) or our "particular moral choices" (Fuchs) do these latter choices take on the character of full freedom. In the core or deep center of the person, every man assumes a *basic choice* (fundamental option) for or against God. Not all his acts share in this fundamental freedom. Using the image of man as multidimensional, we may speak of man's basic choice, which refers to his use of fundamental freedom, in contrast with his various peripheral choices, which involve only a lesser degree of freedom. In his basic choice, man disposes of himself before God and the world in an ultimate, total, and definitive way. His particular or peripheral choices, which concern daily mundane matters, either may manifest or veil this basic choice. For example, our genuine love for the ghetto-dweller may serve as a sign of our basic choice to love God in Christ. On the other hand, a particular choice for a morally evil action harmful to the neighbor (e.g., detraction, calumny, bodily injury) may veil our good basic choice for God, which has not become manifest in this particular choice. Because our basic choice is in principle not amenable to full and certain cognizance, it is only by hoping in God that the Christian accepts freedom without becoming scrupulous or self-righteous. Moral knowledge, understood in this perspective, always implies an implicitly twofold judgment. One concerns the particular moral object or choice which rises to our reflexive and explicit consciousness, e.g.,

"Should I steal this money?" The other judgment refers to the person's ordered response to God who offers himself at this moment in our non-reflexive and implicit (unthematic) consciousness. This latter judgment, which occurs in all our free choices, takes place in the deep center of the person. Moral theology has referred most frequently in the past to the explicit aspect of our moral decisions; the implicit decision now receives great stress. "When St. Thomas says that God is recognized unthematically but really in every object, then this applies equally to freedom: in every act of freedom God is unthematically but really willed and, conversely, one experiences in this way alone what is really meant by God" (K. Rahner, "Theology of Freedom," *Theological Investigations,* Vol. VI, 180).

This free act of radical self-realization before God can only be achieved by means of the individual human acts which can be placed in space and time, yet it cannot be simply identified with such individual acts. Man has the power and the duty to make a reflex and objective judgment about his moral state in his particular acts, but he can never attain absolute certitude about his basic good or evil self through such reflection. One must take account of this knowledge in the calculations of one's life and of one's active decisions, of course, yet it never assumes a final or absolute certainty beyond appeal. On the other hand, skepticism and disregard of our reflexive and critical judgments fail to express our human self-commitment in knowing freedom before God. The importance of our individual choices comes to the forefront, furthermore, when we view man socially, for his concrete choices have immense impact on the lives and choices of other persons. For example, to dismiss the violent act of a revolutionist on the score of his "good faith" or "a basic choice turned toward God" would be to ignore the social implications of human activity and to opt instead for an absolutized individualism. The bomb he throws in "good faith" still kills or maims.

Grace, Faith, Charity and the Fundamental Option

This theory of the fundamental option ties in closely with our understanding of grace. Grace is not a thing, but a movement of life in us. This movement of grace starts in the depths of the eternal love of the Father, which is incarnated and manifested in the love of the Son and communicated through the Spirit. By grace, we are constituted sons in the Son and we discover the necessity of changing our heart from self-centeredness to God-centeredness. This gradual process of deepening our personal relationship with and life-orientation toward God does not occur in one moment, for example, at the first responsible use of reason. Nor does it happen ordinarily through deliberate and abstract reflection. Sometime in his life, however, a person commits himself before the totality of the whole world which confronts him. This commitment most often is only implied in some concrete activity and choice, and so remains only obscurely a conscious decision. The main point is that for the first time he involves himself in the fullness of reality and freely makes a choice which implicitly includes an acceptance or rejection of God, who offers himself through this reality. Only two loves are possible before God who confronts us in the depths of our being; a love of him that is ready to commit oneself to him; or a selfish love which dares to choose self in preference to him. A person either surrenders himself or refuses him, thus imprisoning himself in self-centered love. For St. Augustine and St. Thomas, as for the whole Augustinian and Thomistic tradition about grace, no other fundamental option is possible for an adult. (See P. Fransen, "How Can Non-Christians Find Salvation in Their Own Religions?" in *Christian Revelation and World Religions,* ed. J. Neuner, 67-122.)

Whenever a person opens himself completely and sincerely in an act of faith in God, he implicitly opens his heart to the loving image of the Father, the Word. All faith acts under the movement of charity which is poured forth in the gift of God himself in our hearts through the Spirit. This loving faith implies that a person basically orders his whole life to God through a personal commitment. In current terminology, this process has been termed a "fundamental option," a completely free and dynamic orientation of one's whole life toward the fullness of reality, the center of which is God.

A fundamental option necessarily supposes a personal creed,

that is, some articulated belief. This does not require any systematic or conceptual ordering of truths, but can find its expression in a concrete religious attitude, in a particular way of life, in various symbolic activities, whether suggested by the rites and symbols of any given religion or welling up spontaneously from a person's heart. No person committing himself in this way can do without a personal creed. This deep and existential religious experience of being attracted by the grace of the Spirit toward the living truth of God leads to such a creed, into which a man tries reflexively to express and to translate in those concepts and symbols which are available to him the content and meaning of this profound non-conceptual instinct of faith. This reflection upon the faith-experience remains under the influence of the Spirit, but our complex human psychology cannot escape other dissipating influences. Life tells us that, because of this human complexity, the personal creed in its final formulation may contain false opinions and errors induced by the social and psychological influences of heredity, education and culture, religious environment, and national or social traditions and ways of thought.

These considerations may at least partially clarify some gnawing problems of contemporary man. How can atheists find salvation? How can non-Christians find salvation in their own religions? How can we explain the immense differences in "personal creeds" ascribed to by fervently believing Christians? More particularly, in the context of Christian morality, how does one account for widespread un-Christian and even immoral attitudes (e.g., racial bias, insensitivity to the right-to-life in warfare, social unconcern) which we have all witnessed in some believers? Are atheists and non-Christians outside the possibility of salvation because they do not explicitly acknowledge Christ in faith? Do the un-Christian styles of life and attitudes adopted by some believers necessarily imply a deeper rejection of God who manifests himself in the neighbor? Some insight may be gained from what has already been said about the tension existing in every act of faith. Even the saints and mystics were fully aware of the difference between the authenticity of their mystical experiences and the subsequent interpretation of them which they tried to formulate in either theological concepts or poetic symbols and images (e.g., St. John of the Cross). For the Christian believer, these misinterpretations of his deeper drive toward God are continually corrected by the living Word of the Spirit, as he speaks through the Christian community and in the depths of his heart. Continual confrontation of his thought with the Word of Christ in Scripture, and more so with the living person of Christ in the liturgy, the neighbor, and in prayer links one with the living Truth. Religious and moral truth, viewed in this way, is fundamentally not abstract or conceptual, but rather personal. In the same way, might we not say that many an atheist or non-Christian finds the Christ of faith in the depths of his being, even while rejecting him on the level of explicit, articulated consciousness? Some remarks of Karl Rahner on anonymous Christianity apply here:

> If man accepts the revelation, he posits by that fact the act of supernatural faith. But he also already accepts this revelation whenever he really accepts *himself completely,* for it already speaks in him. Prior to the explicitness of official ecclesiastical faith this acceptance can be present in an implicit form whereby a person undertakes and lives the duty of each day in the quiet sincerity of patience, in devotion to his material duties and the demands made upon him by the persons under his care. What he is then taking upon himself is therefore not merely his basic relationship with the silent mystery of the Creator-God. Accordingly, no matter how he wants to understand and express this in his own reflective self-understanding, he is becoming thereby not merely an anonymous "theist," but rather takes upon himself in that Yes to himself the grace of the mystery which has radically approached us. . . . In the acceptance of himself man is accepting Christ as the absolute perfection and guarantee of his own anonymous movement toward God by grace, and the acceptance of this belief is again not an act of man alone but the work of God's grace which is the grace of Christ, and this means in its turn the grace of his Church which is only the continuation of the mystery of Christ, his permanent visible presence in our history (K. Rahner, "Anonymous Christians," in *Theological Investigations,* Vol. VI, 390-98, at 394).

Fully Human Activity

Some elements of knowledge and freedom must enter into man's activity before we assign to it the note of being human activity. The actions of infants, drunks, or the extremely senile fail to impress us as really human conduct. Normal adults also experience degrees of freedom in their deeds. How might we therefore describe the knowledge and freedom requisite for moral action?

A fully human action would suppose complete *knowledge* of the morality of the proposed action, together with advertence to this moral aspect of the action, and due deliberation before reaching one's actual decision. Spur-of-the-moment decisions hardly qualify as fully human actions, in light of this description. On the other hand, moral activity is not the preserve of intellectual giants. We must not overdo the qualities of normal moral activity. Fully or perfect human activity may seldom be realized; short of this, however, moral actions admit of many degrees. It might be possible for a moralist, for instance, to reason through the ethical intricacies of genetic tampering or transplant operations, while a research clinician or surgeon on the scene grasps only confusedly the full constellation of moral considerations at hand. On the level of practical affairs, this sort of non-technical knowledge often suffices for responsible action. The same holds true for moral matters. Often enough, too, a direct, non-reflexive knowledge will be sufficient, for one could hardly expect people to advert consciously and in detail to the moral aspects of every action they perform. Most people make their ordinary moral decisions with such knowledge. To demand more in the minimal notion of moral action would be to make the ethical life a non-realizable ideal, except for the specialist in ethics and the like.

The knowledge present in our actions must be personalized. A purely theoretical or logical knowledge of moral ideals and values would be something-out-there, an object apart from the person acting. Only when a person appropriates his knowledge by making it his own in personal terms, does there exist *moral* knowledge properly so called. The individual must at least implicitly weigh and evaluate the value of the action in line with his life-orientation toward God. This *evaluative knowledge,* as it has been termed in contradistinction to a merely *conceptual knowledge,* must perdure throughout the action. To the extent that a person fails to evaluate his actions in personal terms, the act does not proceed from himself as master of his life. A deep and intense conceptual and evaluative knowledge is often lacking, but unless such knowledge exists to some degree, properly human action does not occur. The depth and intensity of the act cannot, however, be greater than the depth and intensity of the knowledge of moral value. (See J. Ford-G. Kelly, *Contemporary Moral Theology*, Vol. I, 224-227; J. Fuchs, *Theologia moralis generalis*, pars altera, 1-18, and "Basic Freedom and Morality," in *Human Values and Christian Morality*, 92-111.)

A fully human action must also stem from man's personal center, from the core of his freedom. The act performed must depend on this fundamental decision; otherwise it is imperfectly free, for man does not dispose of himself before God. Spontaneous drives and emotions, and also insufficient or clouded knowledge of the moral value frequently hinder the full use of freedom. Any moral action which proceeds from any degree of freedom, of course, can be called voluntary. Human experience shows, however, the enormous variance in the willingness with which we perform our everyday tasks. "Voluntary" or "free" must assume an analogous and ambiguous connotation to remain true to reality. Between full freedom and total unfreedom lie the normal freedoms we bring to most actions. In the sense explained in previous pages, original or fundamental freedom implies man's total and definitive self-disposal. As with moral knowledge, however, lesser degrees of freedom and decision-making exist which contribute to and support our basic choice. Our self-becoming as a person occurs through these lesser choices which culminate in our basic choice. Our ordinary actions do, then, merit the term "free." They constitute part of that growth *process* of choice leading to a fundamental choice.

The Age for the Basic Choice

A perfect (or grave) moral act implies that a person knowingly and willingly disposes of himself fully and entirely in relationship to God. This life-choice means a complete conversion to God (metanoia), or complete aversion from him (serious sin). In his free and personal core, each person assumes this basic stance before God who offers himself in the depths of our being. When can such a fundamental decision first occur in the life of an average person? The question about the age for this basic choice remains disputed. Negatively, it seems unlikely that a person could achieve such full self-possession based on an awareness of his relationship to God before about the age of puberty. Several conclusions have been drawn from recent research in psychology:

> The age of reason, defined in terms of cognitive development sufficient to enable the child to comprehend concepts, grasp relationships, and understand distinctions, occurs at the onset of adolescence, that is, between eleven and thirteen years of age in almost all children.
> Autonomy of judgment sufficient to make responsible moral decisions manifests itself somewhat later, probably between twelve and fourteen years of age.
> It is clear . . . that moral acts as traditionally viewed demand a level of intellectual development capable of making conceptual, evaluative distinctions consistently. It is also clear that the capacity for thinking in terms of two-way relationships must be present in more than a rudimentary manner. In addition to cognitive maturity, there must be relative autonomy of judgment. The psychological research findings demonstrate that conceptual thinking and autonomy of judgment sufficient for true moral acts *as* currently defined are not present consistently in the average child before twelve or thirteen years of age. The psychological evidence is incontrovertible (R. O'Neil-M. Donovan, *Sexuality and Moral Responsibility* [Washington: Corpus, 1968] 12, 23-24).

The age of puberty, then, would seem to form the lower limits of the human possibility of a personal coming-to-be in an initial grave encounter with God (sometimes called the *optio fundamentalis initialis*). J. Glaser describes the evolving of this choice in terms of two "births" for every person. The first of these is his physical birth; the second is his birth as a genuine person, which occurs through personal commitment. He states:

> The time between the individual's physical birth and his birth in freedom is also a history of encounter with God, but in a way that is qualitatively different from that of the *optio fundamentalis*. Before the individual encounters God in an *optio fundamentalis*, he has passed through a series of

ever-deepening encounters with God on the level of more peripheral freedom. The result of each of these encounters has been a deepened peripheral freedom moving toward the density of core freedom.

Therefore, both the birth of the individual as personal subject and the pre-history of this *optio fundamentalis initialis* must be measured and understood in their ultimate reality as a coming-to-be of the subject insofar as he meets and hands himself over to God. The further stages of the individual's self-realization, following the *optio fundamentalis initialis,* manifest the same structure. Each new deepening of the personal existence that man has "answered-into-being" in his *optio initialis* is, in the last analysis, the result of another encounter with God; it is man existing as the answer he has given, and is, to the new initiative, the new life-giving, self-giving word of God (J. Glaser, "Man's Existence: Supernatural Partnership," *Theological Studies* 30 [1969] 473-88, at 474-75).

Glaser makes reference to Karl Rahner's view on the first grave encounter: "The time between these two births lasts longer, perhaps, than is often supposed. Karl Rahner dares the possibly surprising conjecture: 'Probably the decision of faith which stamps one's total life occurs today as a rule somewhere between the ages of twenty and twenty-five.' " Glaser continues: "It cannot be shown here that the 'personal birth' spoken of above and the decision of faith mentioned by Rahner are the same." Later in his article, however, Glaser offers some serious reasons for equating these two realities.

In conclusion, a fully moral action must embody truly human qualities, knowledge and freedom. Modern psychology has cast doubts on some traditional understandings of man's moral freedom, notably the time for the attainment of the age of reason, once assigned as the age of seven. This classical view does not hold up well when re-examined by psychologists and theologians alike. To question past assumptions about freedom does not, however, make the Christian task of the adolescent any the less strenuous nor the ministry of the Word less demanding. A true freedom exists in the teenager; it must be fostered and challenged toward choosing the service of God, man, and the world, rather than refusing this task by choosing oneself.

The Limitation of Freedom

Fundamental or original freedom refers to the capacity to make oneself once and for all, to dispose of oneself totally and definitively by saying yes or no to God and, by this same fact, to refuse oneself. Even for an adult, however, an individual act of freedom (our many daily acts) may not involve such a full disposal of oneself in these ultimate terms. The person's fundamental freedom (his basic option) may not penetrate entirely his object-choice, and this for a variety of given conditions. The most fundamental of these conditions is contained above all in the implications of the Catholic teaching on original sin and concupiscence (traditionally termed the loss of the gift of integrity). There one sees that created freedom is always conditioned by situations and realizes itself in a world characterized by sin and guilt. There never exists a situation and material for man's freedom which has not been affected by the guilt of sin in the history of mankind. This inherent limitation on freedom makes it less likely that human freedom will be perfectly and finally realized in any single act. The liberating grace of God in the Son must assist the person to open himself in a process of gradual decisions to the fundamental choice of love for God.

Besides this inherent limitation stemming from concupiscence, everything that does not originate in the spiritual self-consciousness of the person may hinder his expressing his original freedom in any given act. His genetic inheritance, environment, culture, habits, traits of personality and sex, health, or sickness, and a variety of psychic states can influence conduct and, at times, endanger the full employment of fundamental freedom. Psychological factors may, for example, conceal an underlying desire to assist other persons with a covering of emotional insecurity. The fundamental choice to act in behalf of other persons may not even emerge into reflexive awareness; the good basic option nevertheless remains. Such traditional impediments as ignorance, emotion, fear, and physical force likewise retain their applicability in a modern theology of human freedom. The influence of the dynamic unconscious and of various psychotic and neurotic states must also enter into any realistic consideration of man's freedom in tune with the findings of modern science. Finally, the social pressures of the technocratic world of today and biological factors (e.g., menopause or general hormonal imbalance) may hinder the concrete realization of personal freedom. Does not the rise of a counter-culture among youth in reaction to modern society exemplify the frustrations of freedom which many experience today?

Awareness of these factors has led many contemporary moralists to question traditional presumptions about freedom. Louis Monden expresses well the significant shift in emphasis that has occurred:

> Classic moral theology contains a treatise, "de impedimentis libertatis" (on the obstacles to freedom), which applies not only within moral doctrine but also within ecclesiastical legislation. It may even, to a great extent, have been transposed from jurisprudence to moral doctrine. A distinction is made between obstacles coming from within, mainly ignorance and the violence of instinctive impulses, and obstacles coming from without, mainly moral coercion, deceit and intimidation (*vis et metus*). In the light of the latest findings, however, these positions appear to be completely outmoded. They take for granted that man's freedom is a perfectly *autonomous power of decision,* hindered in the exercise of its sovereignity only accidentally, by factors which, although possibly often at work, remain by their nature exceptional. Quite different is the picture of man drawn by *contemporary anthropology.* Here human freedom is seen as a freedom in situation, and the dialectic of freedom and determinism is considered essential for every human action. Only this dialectic makes freedom into really human freedom, and modern science seems to find it more difficult to preserve the moment of freedom than to point out all that is determined in man's activity (L. Monden, *Sin Liberty and Law,* 20-21).

Monden cites three main sources—biological, social and psychological—which contribute elements of determinism in man's activity. In-depth treatment of these factors can be found elsewhere, especially in contemporary literature on pastoral counseling. (See the lists of recommended readings in H. Clinebell,

Basic Types of Pastoral Counseling [Nashville: Abingdon, 1966]; also, G. Hagmaier-R. Gleason, *Counseling the Catholic* [N.Y.: Sheed & Ward, 1959]. The six-volume Pastoral Psychology Series available from Fordham University Press under the editorship of W. Bier will prove most useful.)

Despite L. Monden's reservations about classical moral theology's treatise on the obstacles to freedom, we find there some considerations which offer continuing valid insight for thinking in this area and for understanding the moral literature. Classical moral theology spoke of some obstacles which here-and-now hindered man's use of freedom in a given choice. The term "actual impediment" refers to impeding *this* act, in contrast with an "habitual impediment" which, since it stems from habit, impedes all acts or at least acts of a certain kind.

Among the actual impediments, *ignorance,* error and inadvertence would either entirely remove or partially lessen moral responsibility, depending on the degree of knowledge which remains. How could a person choose culpably or inculpably that which he doesn't know? At times, even with the best of good will, people cannot possibly know the correct moral choice, and this *invincible* ignorance totally prevents moral culpability for the wrong choice a person makes. On the other hand, if a person can learn the correct manner of moral behavior and still disregards the ordinary means to seek out this information, his *vincible* ignorance may somewhat lessen guilt, but it will not eliminate it entirely. Many examples of moral ignorance could be cited, especially in connection with cultural factors—lack of moral-religious education, prevailing family or societal moral values—which affect a whole level of society. The need of avoiding a "herd mentality" might well be stressed today. Besides this traditional description of the ignorance which removes or lessens moral responsibility, there sometimes exists an ignorance tied in with the lack of the *evaluative knowledge* described earlier. The person who cannot personalize and evaluate his actions in terms of his response to God, man and the world cannot be considered morally responsible for these actions.

Emotion or passion may have a varied effect on responsibility. Human experience testifies to the vehement way in which anger, joy, sexual attraction, or intense excitement of any sort pervades one's personal grasp of himself and carries him toward decisions never reached in a cooler, more rational frame of mind. Man does not act in a four-storeyed way: intellect, will, emotions, and body. The whole man acts as one; in a real sense, he *is* his emotions and so they animate his concrete actions. In a moral context, strong emotions may lessen responsibility or, less frequently, remove it altogether. Free control based on reasonable motives for action may give way to the judgment of-the-moment and irresponsible activity may eventuate. Real deliberation may hardly occur and freedom disappears. On the other hand, a person's emotional makeup may impel him to spend himself more avidly in the promotion of moral values (for example, a parent who launches out vigorously into an anti-drug campaign in behalf of youth). Given the suspicious overtones regarding the emotions sometimes found in traditional Puritanical or Victorian thinking, it may be in place to recall explicitly their goodness, for every truly human reality is good. (See J. Schaller, *Our Emotions and the Moral Act* [N.Y.: Alba House, 1968].)

Physical or psychic force (fear) may also impair freedom. Man's inner freedom cannot be directly countered, but physical force (e.g., rape) may simply prevent the performance of one's own choice. Any external action done against one's will lacks freedom and moral responsibility. The sphere of psychic force, including fear, dread, and anxiety, seems mysterious and more difficult to assess. Intense fear about some impending danger (e.g., the threat of death to a loved one) can make a free choice impossible. More often, however, ordinary fear lessens somewhat the freedom we bring to our actions. The neurotic dread, anxiety, and other psychic forces referred to in literature on psychology may well diminish moral responsibility in some choices, if not remove it entirely.

Traditional moral theology also recognized the central place of *habit* in man's activities. It is a commonplace to read analyses similar to the following brief statement:

Good habits increase the decisiveness and ease of good actions. On the other hand, a thoughtless act "out of habit," even when it is good by reason of its object, has less freedom about it. Bad habits, in which the weight of preceding mistakes exercises an influence, lessen one's moral freedom to the good, but they do not lessen guilt, as long as the will has embraced the evil aspect of a given act. But when the will, in penance and amendment, has sincerely foresworn a bad habit, a spontaneous outbreak of the old habit, to which one hardly adverts, can be without fault (F. Böckle, *Fundamental Concepts of Moral Theology,* 35).

The principle of diminished moral imputability, whether for good or evil, underlies this approach. At times, a habit may completely remove responsibility, so that the person doesn't actually perform a human action. For example, a person may get so caught up in the habit of lying, stealing or sexual misconduct that he scarcely adverts to the moral dimensions of his conduct; in a sense, he lacks moral sensitivity in the matter. On the other hand, "even when a habit of sin has been contracted deliberately and sinfully, once the habitual sinner repents of the sin involved in contracting the habit, the habit itself is considered involuntary and sinless. This means that hereafter, and as long as he remains in the same good dispositions, the individual acts placed under the influence of habit are no longer attributed to him *in causa.* This means, further, that the formal guilt of any future individual acts, placed under the influence of the acquired habit, must be judged from the individual acts themselves, i.e., according to the amount of effective control he was able to exercise in each instance, considering all the internal and external circumstances of the act. . . . The norms given to measure the extent to which subjective guilt is lessened are not very helpful" (J. Duhamel, "Theological and Psychiatric Aspects of Habitual Sin," *CTSA Proceedings* 11 [1956] 130-49, at 131). According to Duhamel, traditional moral theology contributed little aid "in determining when the intellect's part in the formation of a human act may be considered completely suppressed" (*ibid,* 132). Nor can we accurately determine when habit interferes with freedom in such a way as to impede it totally.

Our visible free acts, limited as they may be by such intellectual, emotional or psychological factors, do not constitute the whole of personal morality. Our previous explanation of fundamental freedom and the kinds of choice associated with this deeper level of man's being points to an area of man's moral life which lies beyond explicit consciousness. At a depth outside reflexive awareness, every man meets the Triune God who offers himself as a gift and a demand. Individual acts of free choice contribute to or hinder that deeper commitment whereby we can grow into that fullness of manhood before the Father which should characterize living in the Spirit of Christ.

BIBLIOGRAPHY

Duhamel, J., "Theological and Psychiatric Aspects of Habitual Sin," CTSA *Proceedings* 11 (1956) 130-49.

Ernst, P., "Option vitale," *Nouvelle Révue Théologique* 69 (1947) 731-42; 1065-84.

Flick, M.-Alszeghy, Z., "L'opzione fondamentale della vita morale e la grazia," *Gregorianum* 41 (1960) 593-619.

Ford, J.-Kelly, G., *Contemporary Moral Theology,* Vol. 1 (Paramus, N.J.: Newman, 1958) 174-312.

Fransen, P., "How Can Non-Christians Find Salvation in Their Own Religions?" in *Christian Revelation and World Religions,* ed. J. Neuner (London: Burns & Oates, 1967) 67-122.

Fuchs, J., "Basic Freedom and Morality," in *Human Values and Christian Morality* (Dublin: Gill and Macmillan, 1970) 92-111.

————, *Theologia moralis generalis,* pars altera (Rome: Gregorian University, 1967) 1-18.

Glaser, J., "Man's Existence: Supernatural Partnership," *Theological Studies* 30 (1969) 473-88.

Jonsen, A., *Responsibility in Modern Religious Ethics* (Wash., D.C.: Corpus, 1968).

McCormick, R., "The Moral Theology of Vatican II," in *The Future of Ethics and Moral Theology* (Chicago: Argus, 1968).

————, "Notes on Moral Theology," *Theological Studies* 27 (1966) 608f.

Maritain, J., *Raison et raisons* (Paris, 1947) 131-65.

————, *Neuf leçons sur les notions premières de la philosophie morale* (Paris, 1949) 119-28.

Monden, L., *Sin, Liberty and Law* (N.Y.: Sheed & Ward., 1965) 19-72.

O'Neil, R.-Donovan, M., *Sexuality and Moral Responsibility* (Wash., D.C.: Corpus, 1968).

Rahner, K., *Theological Investigations,* Vol. IV (Baltimore: Helicon, 1966), 105-20; 169; 180-81; Vol. VI (1969) 231-49; 178-96; 390-98.

Schoonenberg, P., *Man and Sin* (Notre Dame Univ., 1965).

Sikora, J., "Faith and First Moral Choice," *Sciences Ecclésiastiques* 17 (1965) 327-37.

Index of Subjects

Index of Proper Names